Look Again ... Because Y al
journey, personal comm le
Jones as a survivor of dc ...le
sharing her journey, the book provides perspectives from
those who love her. As they discuss their thoughts and feelings about the abuse going on in Neile's life, Neile shares
how those around her helped her through her experience.
Neile's story is a reminder that domestic violence can—
and does—happen to anyone. It also provides a unique
insight into what friends and family can do to assist a person walking through this painful and unfortunately all-
too-common situation.

—Kim Wells, Executive Director, Corporate
Alliance to End Partner Violence

Neile's family joined the Boston Avenue United
Methodist Church in Tulsa, Oklahoma, when she
was nine years old. Three years later, I had the privilege of confirming her in the faith of her parents and
grandparents. I have been her pastor and her family's
pastor all these years since that time. I saw her grow up,
mature, and move out into the world with such beauty,
intellect, poise, and purpose. I had no idea that she was
a victim of domestic abuse. I am honored to have been
given the opportunity to read her manuscript of that
experience and how she has triumphed over it in such a
wonderful way. It is my prayer that her story will encourage as many others as possible to see a way forward for
them that is equally positive and life-affirming.

—Rev. Dr. Mouzon Biggs, Jr., Senior Minister, Boston
Avenue United Methodist Church in Tulsa, Oklahoma

It is difficult to be transparent about life's challenges. Neile's willingness to share her very personal story is a testament to her courage and a message of hope to those who find themselves in similar circumstances. I am proud to be her friend and inspired by her determination to build a new life filled with love and support for so many others.

—Elise Mitchell, President and CEO,
Mitchell Communications Group

Here is a must-read for those who suffer in silence and see no light at the end of the tunnel. Neile serves as a wonderful beacon to those who believe they are trapped in an abusive relationship. She is kind and courageous and has found true joy. Know that all who pick up this book deserve the same. Read it and begin the rest of *your* amazing life.

—Coleman and Shirley Peterson,
Partners, Hollis Enterprises, LLC

LOOK AGAIN
BECAUSE YOU CAN

NEILE JONES-BATIE

LOOK AGAIN
BECAUSE YOU CAN

TATE PUBLISHING & *Enterprises*

Published by Tate Publishing & Enterprises, LLC
127 E. Trade Center Terrace | Mustang, Oklahoma 73064 USA
1.888.361.9473 | www.tatepublishing.com

Tate Publishing is committed to excellence in the publishing industry. The company reflects the philosophy established by the founders, based on Psalm 68:11,
"The Lord gave the word and great was the company of those who published it."

Published in the United States of America

ISBN: 978-1-61663-319-6
Family & Relationships: Abuse: Domestic Partner Abuse
10.04.27

Dedication

This book is dedicated to my family. Thank you for loving me and allowing me the freedom to find myself without judgment. This book would not be possible without you and your support. You are a blessing in every way.

Table of Contents

13   Foreword

15   Preface

19   Hello

25   Here We Go

27   How Did I Get Here?

49   Where Do I Go from Here?

63   The Work Is Just Beginning

83   Make a Difference

99   You're Light

103   From Father to Father

107   From Mother to Mother

111   From Sister to Sister

115   From a Friend before and After

119   A Word from My Husband

123   Neil Diamond Moment

127   Thank You

137   Journal

147   Helpful Resources

Foreword

Abuse, unfortunately, is all too common in our society. As a Congressman from the Third District of Arkansas, I have seen the ongoing work being done to combat the problem and help victims of this violence, educate to prevent future abuse, and the assistance available in crisis-intervention services. As much as the position of a lawmaker can help to resolve issues, the real inspirational stories and support come from the people who lived through these terrible situations. Having the strength and courage to come forward to share stories of survival is inspirational, and we are blessed that Neile is sharing her experience. I have met many memorable and remarkable people of all walks of life. Early in my career I had the privilege of meeting Neile, who was interviewing me for a news story. She had everything going for her—her good looks, great voice, and larger-than-life personality. I enjoyed getting to know her through subsequent interviews. She always struck me as the type of person who seems so in control and confident. Neile proves that things aren't always as they appear. Little did I realize the drama that was going on in her life with a very unhappy and abusive relationship. Luckily, Neile was able to get out of the cycle of abuse. She illustrates just how common the problem is and how difficult it is to deal with, while also showing the hope in being able to overcome the circumstances and move on with life. This is a tale of courage and hope, with expert advice on how to cope from someone who understands because she lived through it. Thanks to Neile for having the courage and desire to come forward so that others might follow her example, and for being part of the solution.

—U.S. Congressman John Boozman
3rd District of Arkansas

Neile Jones-Batie

Preface

I believe life is about choices. Where you end up is a reflection of where you've been and the decisions you've made that allowed you to become an achiever. I have been blessed with a wonderful family and a rewarding career in the broadcast television industry. As general manager of an NBC affiliate in northwest Arkansas, I met a young woman with a lot of potential. Being new to the area, I didn't know much about her, but I quickly realized she had recently experienced some problems in her personal life. I didn't know how deep her wounds were until much later.

Recognizing talent is part of my job. Neile Jones had talent, although she wasn't ready to realize it. In mid-2004, I asked Neile to meet with me. I had an opening for a main anchor position, and I offered her the opportunity. This would be a high-profile position in a community that was rapidly growing. What you see in someone is not always what they see in themselves. I was handing Neile a chance of a lifetime. She handed it right back and said,

"No." It was then I realized I was looking at a person who was deeply hurt and brokenhearted.

She didn't know what she wanted. She thought her pain would be lessened if she could escape a town that caused it. She wanted to start fresh. I had to step back and think about the situation. Some people think running from something will make you stronger. In reality, running toward it enables you to heal. Several days later, I met with Neile again. I believed in her abilities. I wanted her to believe in herself. What happened next set the stage for success and began a personal friendship that I will treasure forever.

Sometimes you have to go with your gut. My gut was telling me to speak frankly to this fragile individual sitting in front of me. I didn't know where I was going with this, but I did know that no was not an option, so I went with it. I told her we needed to talk about her future—again. "This is about your future, not about your past," I said. "You have to believe in yourself. This is an excellent opportunity for you. As your general manager, I love you. You do a great job. For you, though, you need to get a life." This was my attempt to shake her at the core. It seemed the only male figure she trusted at the time was her dad. "Neile, take some time and think about this opportunity. Drive to Tulsa tomorrow and talk to your parents." I knew they were the only people who could influence her in her current state. She needed confidence. A couple days later, confidence walked into my office. "You're right" is what I heard. "I have decided to take you up on your offer," she said. I was thrilled. In the weeks that followed, I would look up and see Neile coming in the back door two or three hours before her shift, in her workout attire. She was taking control of her life. Dropping some pounds and getting in shape was next on her list. It got to the point I would be walking down the hall and I would look up to see black spandex shorts and hear a friendly, "Hi there." Neile was getting a life.

The key to success with local broadcast television stations is to have a commitment to the community you serve. Neile focused her energies on several non-profit groups. She volunteered her free time to lend assistance to people who had fallen on hard times. We used the power of television to relay that commitment to the community. This wasn't something I asked her to do. I stood next to her and gave her support to allow the television station to be her bullhorn. It did nothing but get louder. Neile was alive. Neile was believing in people again when only a short time ago, she was unable to believe in herself. Neile always spoke about her grandmother. I learned her grandmother was a breast cancer survivor. Neile continued to increase her commitment to the community. This time it was the Susan G. Komen Foundation. She and I worked together to create a platform whereby she could raise awareness and education about breast cancer in Northwest Arkansas. We knew if we could save one life, it would be worth it. The first step in this process came with "Team Neile." Viewers were urged to join Neile's team to participate in the local Race for the Cure event. This was only the beginning. Six months later, we created Project 11. This was a program that not only educated people about breast cancer, but encouraged friends to remind friends about self-examination for early detection. Neile was everywhere. Anywhere she could get an audience, people had to listen. She was working all the time. This was her calling. She became someone who couldn't say no.

Neile is an amazing person.

To know someone who experiences suffering at the hands of someone she made a commitment to is something I still don't understand. I will never know the depth of pain she experienced. I will also never understand what makes a man think he has the right to inflict mental and physical abuse on a woman. Life is about choices. Those choices make us winners or losers. Neile is the winner. Her experiences made her stronger.

I can't express to you how proud I am of her. I am thrilled to have the opportunity to tell you about my friend. Before you turn this page, always know you can remember, but never look back. Enjoy this look ahead.

—Blake Russell
Senior Vice President
Nexstar Broadcasting

Hello

Neile Jones at KNWA Studio in Fayetteville, Arkansas

I am Neile Jones, a news anchor in Northwest Arkansas for the NBC affiliate. I've worked in the market for some thirteen years as an anchor/reporter/producer. In that time I have lived my dream. I have also lived my worst nightmare. I have tried to live my life as best I can. I have made mistakes, poor choices, and lived with the consequences. I have also learned from my road, a path that brought me to a wonderful place in life, a place where I am finally comfortable in my own skin, with who I am, where I've been, and where I hope to go.

God has blessed me through good times and bad. I have found angels along the way—people placed in my life to offer me encouragement and support at just the right time so I keep moving toward my dreams. As I continue to learn about myself and what I hope to become, I have discovered that what I feel is something we all learn in life. It's simple. If you truly let yourself see, then you can and will find your way. Let me explain.

My father taught me at a young age that sometimes we have to close our eyes to see our vision. Sometimes the only way you can really understand is in the quiet of the night, when you're alone with your thoughts. No TV. No radio. No distractions. Just you closing your eyes so you can grasp the images that are right in front of you. I have learned to believe in what seems unattainable and impossible. Dream big and play hard. I believe that if you let yourself see your vision, you can and will do anything, be anything, help anyone, achieve the impossible, and become a believer in what the world sometimes forgets. What's impossible only remains that way if you let it. You can help someone you don't know with a simple word or act of kindness. Look at me. Thousands have watched me over the years. But few know what I am about to share. This book is my dream, my hope to continue helping myself and others because I believe I can. I believe we can. I believe you can help yourself and those around you. You don't have to be a genius or have millions of dollars to make a difference. What I have learned is that sometimes it's best to start by helping yourself.

I want to share my story with you in an effort to help open up the lines of communication about domestic violence. I hope my thoughts will serve as a tool in the healing process for myself and for others. I know that everyone's story is different. I also know there are people who have had much more difficult times and people who have had a much easier time of it. But we all have our struggles. We all have our own paths to walk. What I learned on my walk is that I've never been alone. I may have felt alone, but God was and is with me. My family and friends all watched me and helped me in their own way. For some, that meant taking a step back, allowing me to make mistakes. For others, it meant giving me a safe place where I could be still enough to melt into my own thoughts and sort though the memories that would quietly haunt me until I faced them. Some came and helped me pack my bags; others hid me while putting a roof over my head and offering me a place to sleep without the constant fear of who or what might come through the door. Like a butterfly in a cocoon, God and my family surrounded me with a safe nest, allowing me to prepare to spread my wings and fly.

I am just a woman who wants to share what I've learned while continuing to learn from others. I am also a woman who wants to say that I am not what or who you would expect. I'm not even what I expected. I am a survivor of an abusive relationship—an angry dance that almost took my sight and stole my heart. If you get nothing else from the words on these pages, please take this thought with you:

If you think abuse is not happening to someone you know, look again. You could be very wrong. Look again because you can know someone in an abusive relationship, you can help, you can get help, and you can move on. You may have a friend right now who needs your help and doesn't express it because she is scared—scared of harm, scared of judgment, scared of what she knows and you don't; scared that no one understands why she stays or why she keeps going back. A person living in a world that prevents him or her from seeing the truth because the truth hurts too much. It's a fear that most people find hard to grasp. You can help. She can help herself, but she may need some assistance when it comes to finding her strength again. And if you are that person, don't give up.

On the pages that follow, you'll notice I won't name the man who hurt my family and me. There are several reasons behind that act. He is not the point. Blame is not the point. Breaking the cycle, learning from each other, and getting better—that is our focus here.

If you are reading this book hoping to hear the gory details of a sordid affair, you will be sorely disappointed. But if you are seeking knowledge or support, my hope is that you will find what you need on the pages that follow. I am far from perfect. I am a Christian, a wife, a sister, a daughter, a friend, and a sinner. I am also someone who has been blessed even during the most difficult of times. I imagine we are similar in many ways, just as we are different in many ways.

But you and I are special in the same way. We are God's creatures. God sees us and our sparkle that twinkles of him in our hearts, and that is what makes all of us special. We are blessed with all that life entails. Sometimes we do get in our own way, but if we listen with all of our senses, the truth behind our mistakes can offer us answers we never thought possible.

And last but not least, I have made mistakes. I am not innocent in this situation. We all have to take responsibilities for our judgments and actions. I tried hiding; I tried fighting back. I've cursed and fought back in self-defense and tried to find something to free me. I've curled up and waited for the next blow that may or may not come. I finally wised up and left a place that offered me nothing but darkness. How? With the help of people like you. With God's help. With my will to see and my belief in the right to happiness, a right we all have.

Remember, I am not an expert or a professional licensed to handle these types of situations, so if you are in an abusive relationship, please seek help by contacting the proper authorities and professionals.

Here We Go

I have heard so many people say, "I've never known any-one who's been in a violent relationship," or better yet, the people who say, "I don't understand why someone would stay with a person who hits them." Yeah, you fill in the blank. And when you do, remember that, my friends, is a dangerous assumption, one I understand all too well because I've been on both sides of that statement.

I used to be one of those people. I did stories about abuse. I spent hours on the phone getting the details of different cases involving abuse. I talked with men and women who were trying to recover from a situation that had left them with black and blue marks. I interviewed doctors and nurses and talked with investigators and attorneys. I learned about rape kits and talked with detec-tives. I interviewed men and women with bruises and deep scars. All this without noticing what I was dealing with at home. Isn't it funny how all of us can seem to see others, but when we look at ourselves, it isn't that easy?

One day I closed my eyes while standing in front of my bathroom mirror. When I opened them, I saw a woman I didn't know—a hollow person with no sparkle, no life inside; an empty shell trying to protect its dead contents from those who might see the truth. I felt as though all I could see in the reflection was a whole lot of nothing and no one, an identity someone had slowly carved out of what used to be me. In that moment, I started to understand that my life had to change. I was scared, confused, ashamed, shocked, disappointed, and in a daze. There aren't enough adjectives to describe that feeling or that hurt. I remember looking at finger bruises on my arms and marks on my legs. Here is the scary part: I made excuses because I didn't have any marks on my face. He was smart that way. I was about to get smarter.

How Did I Get Here?

Now that's the question many don't want to ask, mainly because the answer usually includes admitting to their role in the demise of their person. Trust me; I know. I had to ask myself that very thing: *How did I get here?* I didn't get my answer overnight. In fact, I worked hard with a counselor who helped me open up to myself. I continue to work to this day. I have found a lot of tough answers and found out many things about myself for which I have to accept responsibility and choose to change. One of those things: I choose not to be a victim anymore, and so can you.

If you are asking yourself, "How did I get here?" and it's not for some great accomplishment that you are being way too humble about, then you should probably consider professional help. Yes, I am referring to some type of counseling. A licensed therapist can be the key to conquering fears and learning from past mistakes. I believe if you are afraid to face yourself, you'll make up excuses to avoid getting help. You may not even realize what you are doing because you're so lost that you've convinced yourself to believe in the fiction you've written. But why should we not find ways to be better human beings no matter what our situation? I mean, let's think about this. If your business has a problem, you hire someone from the outside to help you rectify the situation. That consultant may make suggestions and observations, but in the end, you make the choices and you do the work. When you need help with food choices, you ask a nutritionist. When you want to get in shape, you call a trainer or go to a gym. Why not ask an expert to help you look more closely at the inner workings of you and your choices? Your bottom line is more important than any financial statement.

You have choices. I had choices. So did my friends, and so did my family. My bad choices led me down the wrong path. I know it and deal with it. It helps a lot when you're back on the right path.

The mirror is the beginning of a choice. When what you see in the reflection is unrecognizable and almost too much to bear, you keep looking but close your eyes. When you are giving yourself the "what happened to the person I used to know," it stinks on every level. I know what it's like to be hit by the very person who says "I love you" hours later—a scary and unfortunate reality for anyone. I also know what it means to run, hide, fight back, yell, cuss, grab, and scream out of fear, self-defense, and exhaustion. I know regret. I know what it's like to say and do nothing because any response could be, will be, and somehow is wrong, and that means later you can expect to be punished. You will either suffer passive aggressively or outright. Your pet will be threatened, your things destroyed, and finally your person.

None of this just happens overnight, yet at the same time, you don't remember or see when the process began, at least not until you're ready.

I remember asking myself, "What just happened?" and, "How did this happen to me?" I also remember asking God for a sign, but I was asking for something I already had.

My mother and father never wanted this life for me. They did their best to teach me to believe in me and choose better. They helped me find my light inside, but I got myself into this mess.

I don't know why we try rationalizing things we know make no sense. I had the very sign—*signs*—I needed. I mean, what more do you need than marks on your body. I kept telling myself, *Hey, I haven't been hit or had a bruise on my face, so the situation isn't that bad.* It doesn't matter. All of that stuff is crapola as I like to say. I know that now, but at the time I just couldn't seem to wrap my mind around or accept that I had become a part of what my counselor calls the "angry dance."

Richard, as we will call him, would often walk by during these moments and say something to the effect of, "You sure got yourself banged up." Or if he was having one of his more sensitive moments, it would be a lame apology followed by, "I never wanted to hit you," a statement I so desperately wanted to believe. So I did. It's hard to understand why people put up with this, unless you've been through that type of pain. I started to believe it was my fault. I have to say to an extent, it was and will always be my fault. I kept going back. I started saying "I'm sorry" at the end of every sentence, a habit I still fight.

Please understand that this situation is a slow, brain-washing-type process that an abuser accomplishes, and quite frankly, I helped by empowering his acts. I kept silent. I covered my marks. I thought I was being strong. As someone who's survived that type of situation, I have to admit there is a kind of strength in trying to just keep going, trying not to allow someone to hold you back from professional dreams even if he or she has already stolen your personal dreams. A hard reality is knowing that while I asked people to come forward with their stories, I was living this lie. It was a façade that would eventually fade away until there wasn't even a shadow of the Neile Jones my family once knew. If I couldn't see my true self, how could they?

We started out like happy couples do, I guess, but even then there were signs I subconsciously chose to ignore when we were dating. Or maybe I just didn't know or want to look for them yet—subtle hints of a life to come that I didn't want to see because I wanted to believe that this man was "the one" for me. I've made a list of some things that stand out to me now as I look back on the situation. By no means am I saying these things will be true for everyone as warning signs, but they made what I call my "gut check" go off; that internal alarm that tells you when something's just not right. I just kept silencing it until I ignored it so long I lost belief in that built in gut warning system. Don't lose yours, ladies. Your internal alarm is a gift from heaven. It's there for a reason, and if you turn it off, only you can turn it back on.

Take a look at the list below of some things I think my senses told me to pay attention to but I, for some reason, ignored. Maybe you'll recognize some of them, or maybe you will just be more aware of them.

1. Telling me he had been accused of abuse by others

2. Jealousy about people and things

3. Lying

4. Resentment toward anyone or anything I cared about or who cared about me, especially my family

5. Road rage

6. Flip-flopping personality

7. Quietly controlling

8. Cruelty to animals

Let's break it down.

1. Telling me he had been accused of abuse by others:

Richard told me about fights he had had and people who had accused him of hitting—a former wife and a girl-friend. Why did I not run the other direction right then and there? I used to be a blindly positive person, mean-ing all I heard was a man being honest, right? I mean, he wouldn't tell me if there was any truth to what those ladies had said. Wrong. Richard was setting the stage for a lifetime of twisting the truth and manipulating the facts until they became so warped in his mind that his fiction became his fact.

I muted my internal alarm and used his charm as the excuse. Charm can go a long way, but watch out for false charm. I fell for it, and I got burned by it. I, of course, believed everything I heard from Richard. I guess I just wanted to believe he was everything I wanted. I wanted to help him see who he was down deep so he wouldn't be afraid of getting hurt. I wanted to believe I could be the good in his life that he'd never had. What I failed to understand was that people make decisions, and when they make poor ones repetitively, the action can lead to a pattern. Those other ladies were a warning of what was yet to come. Soon, the two of us together were nothing more than a potion full of poison.

2. Jealousy about people and things:

Jealousy is an ugly thing. I think everyone is guilty of jealousy about something. But when jealousy becomes a weapon or something you can't quickly snap yourself out of, you have a big ball of ugly trouble. I remember some friends throwing me a surprise birthday lunch. It was such a morale booster at the time, a small thing that seemed to breathe life in me. We had so much fun and laughed. It was nice to have people care about my birthday. Of course, Richard couldn't let me be happy about that for very long. In fact, at one point, I asked Richard if he knew about the surprise birthday lunch. He said yes, but, "You don't need that much attention." He couldn't stand the idea that a small group of friends had done something for me just because it was my birthday. Soon, Richard started to resent people if they said they'd watched me on television. Even when his own friends or coworkers said something to that effect, later he would let me know it was fake and those people were really making fun of me. I was "crazy" to believe anyone really meant anything positive said to me. I didn't understand it then, but now I can see he said those things because any flattery that I received and he didn't meant he wasn't winning the game he was playing in his mind. Our relationship for him was more of a competition with me than two people living life as a team that would allow both of us to succeed. His jealousy didn't end there. He would get upset with me if I went to the gym for a workout because he was sure I was there for someone else. The idea I was working out for me wasn't something he could allow.

Looking back, I believe he was jealous because he knew what he was doing when he wasn't with me. His jealousy centered on his knowledge of his own weaknesses and broken promises.

3. Lying:

Okay, yes, everyone has told a lie. Anyone who says he or she has never told a lie is probably lying. But it was the things Richard lied to me about. I remember he took a work trip with his boss once. I thought it was so sweet that he called me and told me good night and that he loved me. Later I learned that was an act for his boss. He lied about people he worked with, how much he was drinking, where he was going, or where he had been. He took long lunches that made no sense. He told me stories about the women in his office and how they would hit on him.

But his lies eventually spread. For example, I remember him calling me to pick him up from a party. He said he'd had too much to drink and wanted me to come get him. When I got to the party, friends were saying, "Neile, let him stay." He kept telling them, "I don't know why she is here," as if to insinuate I was trying to be a fun hater. I finally said, "He called me to come and get him," and went on to say something like, "You guys have no idea what he is like the day after a drunken night like this. I'll be the one who pays for this night of fun." Looking back, I can't believe I said that out loud. But I did. I'm not sure if that was smart or an ignorant act of defiance, me just fed up with his crap.

The list goes on and on. The sad part was that I always fell for the lie, and he took great pleasure in making sure I knew I had been "stupid" when I believed him. The act of the lie served several purposes. It made me doubt my ability to trust anything. And I believe it gave him great pleasure to know that each lie caused me pain, giving him more control over my life. These were calculated moves to make me doubt myself and to chip away at any self-confidence I might have left.

4. Resentment toward anyone or anything I cared about or who cared about me, especially my family:

My family says they heard from me less and less. I used to go home at least once or twice a month. In fact, at some points I went home almost every weekend I think because

I knew Richard wouldn't go home with me. But then as the relationship became more entangled and intense, I would avoid the people I loved the most. He picked fights with people he knew were important in my life. If I had a close friend, he would come up with some reason that friend wasn't good for me. These were not things said or done out of love. These actions and words came with a fierce intent, hidden from everyone. The goal: get me to the point where Richard was the only person who mattered in my life in the unhealthiest way. It got to the point Richard thought anyone who was a friend was just a person who used me. He even hated my dog—yep, my sweet dog.

Neile Jones-Batie and Phong

At times he would say, "I'm gonna slit that dog's throat if you go to work." So Phong would go to work with me and either sit on my feet during the newscast, go to a friend's, or sleep in my car with water and open windows during the show. Again, none of this happened in one day. It happened slowly and in spurts. And there was almost always an "I'm so sorry. I won't do that ever again." Followed by tears, hugs, tenderness, and promises of a life, I still needed to believe was within our grasp. I know now those words and acts were simply time tools for Richard. He knew each "I'm sorry" bought him a little more time. And with every second I became a little more his.

5.   Road rage:

I remember driving down the road, and then all of sudden he was cussing and screaming at the person in the car behind us. Richard kept flipping the car off and screaming at the other driver to pull over. Then all of a sudden, Richard pulled our car onto the shoulder of the highway. He jumped out and headed to the car behind us, where he tried to entice the teenager to get into a fistfight on the side of the road. Oh yes! He was a big, strong man. I was humiliated and kept thinking, *Please get him back in the car. Please get us home and don't let anyone get hurt.* It was humiliating, and there was no explaining to Richard how unnecessary this roadside scene was and is. He did this several times. And I noticed that each time I said less and less. I knew that any fight picked with a person around us meant a fight with me later if I tried to settle Richard down. A fight with me meant more injuries to hide and more pain to conceal.

6. Flip-flopping personality

Okay, does this really need an explanation? Just in case, the answer is yes. One minute this man wanted to profess his love for me, beg me to have his children, tell me I was the best thing that ever happened to him. Buy me gifts and send me flowers. The next, he was telling me how worthless I was and how much people hated me; how if it wasn't for Richard, no one would talk to me.

It became so extreme that many times he would say something hateful to me just before we walked into a room full of people. Once we were in the room, he would be so kind and loving; I would think everything was going to be okay. Then once we left the party or the room full of friends, he would flip a switch in his mind and every ounce of anything gentle disappeared. Those moments were the ones that often caused the most pain. The limbo of trying to understand in my mind what was the real relationship and what was the closing act to a great show.

7. Quietly controlling:

I slowly learned that Richard's way was the only way. Now, I am referring to something beyond the norm of getting to know a person's habits and how your habits differ. This isn't about how a shirt is folded. Richard got into the habit of telling me he wouldn't care if I died. I don't mean he told me in the heat of the moment of a fight. I mean, just before we'd walk out the door to meet friends or right when we got home, Richard would look at me and say, "I don't think I'd notice for weeks if you were dead." He would follow it up with something along the lines of, "I wouldn't care if you died," or, "I was in the military, and they train us not to care about that." His whole face changed in those moments. It was as if his eyes became lumps of coal with no warmth, just cold. He wasn't screaming at me. He was calm, cool, and collected, which put a chill down my spine every time because it was almost as though he was thinking out loud and I knew the directions his thoughts were headed. His voice changed, and he made sure he was making direct eye contact with me. It scared me to death every time. I would then try to make myself as invisible as possible. He wanted me to disappear, and he wanted to make sure I understood his deep hatred for me and anything and everything to do with me. Every move I made was a defensive tactic, forcing me into what I call a kind of survival mode. I knew the unspoken rules. Confining to those rules was a slow torture that I didn't even see happening until it was too late. The rules started out simple enough: Never leave a light on in the house, even if it's because you don't want to walk into a dark house when you come home. Never speak the truth. Only say what Richard wants to hear. Move out of the way if he is going to pass you in the hallway, or he will move you into the wall. Don't walk through a door too slowly if he wants you to hurry, or you will be shut so hard in the door you'll get a bruise you'll be hiding for weeks. When his football team plays, if they lose, don't speak; lock yourself in a different room with your dog (Phong). If you don't, you'll be hit in the head with a football while he takes out his frustrations on you and anything that you care about. Don't talk to your friends on the phone in a room where he can't hear what's being said. If he wants the couch, you better sit on the floor. Don't try to share the couch with him. And when he drinks and wants to drive, know that taking the keys from him or stopping him means you're the enemy, even though you are really just trying to keep him from hurting anyone else. I knew to make our relationship appear wonderful on the outside so that when we got wherever we were headed, I might be safer when the room emptied and we were alone. I look back and still wonder how I was able to go into survival mode and make myself a ghost of a person before I was able to tell my family the truth. Not necessarily survival mode to get out of the situation, at least not yet. The audacity of his tactics became increasingly more effective as I lost any sense of self.

8.   Cruelty to Animals

I believe this is a huge indicator of a person's character and moral compass. We had two dogs between the two of us. Richard had gotten one dog before I met him. In fact, he seemed to love this dog so much. He would bring him places and love on him…sound familiar? One time I remember one of the dogs was locked in the bathroom with the lights out and he was whining. I had never seen anyone do this before, so I asked Richard what was going on. The response was, "He s*** in the house, so now he's being punished." I made the mistake of saying "But how does he understand what he did wrong if it happened when you weren't home?" Richard flung open the bathroom door, grabbed the dog by the neck, and threw him into the living room by his neck. I don't mean he grabbed the dog by the extra skin on the back of the dog's neck. I mean he grabbed the dog, putting both hands around the animal's neck, and threw him into the next room. No, he didn't toss him. He threw this dog, and the poor thing kept yelping in pain. I had never seen anyone treat an animal this way. I was so shocked I froze and looked at the dog then looked at Richard. As I started to cry, Richard began walking back toward this poor dog that couldn't have weighed more than fifty pounds. I put myself between him and the dog. He cooled off, and then, just like he would soon begin doing with me, started saying, "I never meant to hurt him." This was the first time I'd seen anyone really act like this with an animal. Richard kept saying, "I've never done that before. I'm so sorry." This act of violence happened before I was ever hit. But just as he became more violent toward me, over time I believe the same was true for the pets.

One day when Phong was pretty young, probably not more than a year old and not full grown, I came home from work, and as soon as I walked past Richard he said, "I beat the s*** out of that dog today," Knowing Phong was a puppy and hoping for the best, I said, "That's not funny." He said, "I'm not kidding." I said, "What are you talking about?" Richard's response was, "He chewed the hose in half, so I beat him with this," simultaneously showing me the hose as if to brag about his conquest over a helpless and defenseless puppy. I dropped all my bags and went running to the backyard. Phong was in a corner, curled up and scared. I called him, but he wouldn't come, so I walked over and scooped him up with almost no response from him, which is very abnormal. Richard came walking toward us with the hose, yelling and laughing. Phong started clawing to get out of my arms, obviously scared of the man walking toward us.

I would only truly realize the damage done as time went on because from that day on, if a hose was in the backyard, the dog wouldn't walk near it. You could literally watch him make a huge, nervous, and hesitant circle to avoid going near the hose.

Yeah, the puppy chewed through a hose left out by a man who knew better than to leave it out. Who's really at fault here, the puppy or the man who didn't put up the hose? For a dog to remember something like that for so many years after it happened, I know that was a severe beating, and I know it for more than one reason. I know it as I sit here typing these words and wiping tears from my face. The way Richard treated animals was something that escalated just like the way he treated me.

After this happened, Phong started going with me more and more. If I locked myself in a room, then I locked Phong in the room with me. Eventually Phong grew into his own, and in fact, both dogs, if inside, would eventually get between me and Richard in the darkest of moments because they were trying to protect me.

I still live with the thought that I put Phong in harm's way. I live with the fact I couldn't take the other dog with me. I live with memories of two dogs showing me love and compassion and never judging me while at the same time getting punished by a person who professed to love them and all animals.

I never thought anything like that would ever happen. For Phong, I can say it never happened again. I can also say these were signs, hints, all warnings that I couldn't see because I was too engrossed in the idea of repairing a relationship that was doomed to fail. But in this case, that may not be a bad thing.

Again, I know people who say, "I don't understand why a woman stays in an abusive relationship." I hope you never know. The reason for that lack of understanding is a lack of experience. I had to know I'd done all I could to make things work. Believe me; I did a lot of praying and even more soul searching. I spent many nights in a Methodist church searching for solitude and answers through prayer. On several Sundays, I would drive to Tulsa and sit in the back of the church where I grew up when it was empty in the afternoon. For some reason, I felt I didn't deserve anything different. But here is the deal. We all deserve peace in our relationships. We just have to see that right as a reality, meaning the person we love has to be treated with love and respect, as do we. I know people fight, but there is definitely a difference between healthy fighting and abuse.

After months of this, I knew something was wrong, but I couldn't seem to find my footing. I couldn't seem to see what I needed to do next. I also hate to admit this, but a part of me didn't want to admit I had picked someone so wrong for me. I picked someone who, in reality, seemed to hate me in private and love me in public. I began to despise myself and resent what I'd become. It took me a while to figure that out, but when I did, it broke my heart.

In the beginning, we were great, for the most part, when people were around. He was, for all practical purposes, sweet, kind, and attentive. But as time went on, that changed to the polar opposite.

One night, after a huge argument, I called my sister. That phone call was the beginning of the rest of my life. In fact, I must credit Holly. She did something no one else could do. She got me to close my eyes and see a piece of me I'd forgotten. Let me explain.

When I called my sister, I was frantic. I wasn't crying because my feelings had been hurt. I was crying because I was fighting myself to say something to her, tears streaming down my face, a frustration of fear, hurt, and a fatigue combined with displaced loyalty to a person who only wanted to hurt me. I wanted to say, "Holly, come get me." I wanted to say, "Holly, he's hurting me." I couldn't put together all the phrases that were going through my head. I didn't know how much time I had. I was almost out of breath by the time she answered the phone. I told her that Richard and I had just had a big fight. She asked me what happened, and I said, "I can't tell you." I told her I was worried she wouldn't forgive him. A deafening and defining silence followed. But moments later, my sister knew exactly what to say and how to get me to listen.

I'll never forget her response: "Neile, what if I told you Kevin [her husband] and I had a fight and I couldn't tell you what happened because you might not forgive him?" I knew what she meant. This type of thing goes beyond the normal private conversations kept between a couple. I would never tolerate a situation I thought was leaving my sister injured physically and/or mentally. I couldn't stand the thought of someone hurting my sister, and I would find it unacceptable for my sister, just as it was unacceptable for me.

Now, understand, I was feeling my sister out. Did she already know my secret? Did she think it was all my fault? In that moment, she let me know she cared without judging me. She also let me know she was aware something was going on that should never happen. She wanted happiness for me. That conversation marked my first steps toward a belief that I did deserve more.

I wish I could say I left the relationship immediately, but I can't. That's the bad news. The good news is, for the first time I began to understand the seriousness of my situation. I started to understand that a man who said things like, "I'll slit your dog's throat if you go to work," or, "I wouldn't notice if you died" wasn't the man for me. A man who said, "Good, I hope I knocked you out" wasn't good enough. I know everyone says things when angry, and those words can be taken out of context. But Richard seemed to say cruel things more and more. His words became more violent in nature, and I became more a believer in his threats. I also became the butt of his joke when we were around people. But *we* weren't laughing; he was. I learned to put on a good face for others and play the "good sport" role. Now, don't get me wrong. I would spout off back at him, but eventually my confidence changed. I stopped the preverbal banter that eventually led to a huge fight later. I wasn't allowed to tease him back. I wasn't allowed to stand up for myself. This became a survival technique.

A combination of things happens when you're scared. You try to be strong and protect yourself by protecting the delicate situation that's now become your life. Even more perplexing is the instinct to protect the very person who hurts you. Another problem was that on some level, I started to believe him every time he said, "Your friends don't really like you." I also began to see the extremes I had to go to in order to hide the truth of my situation from others. This was a dangerous time because I was starting to see the reality of my situation, and I wasn't equipped to recover from my descent. I was spiraling, and the only place I felt safe was when I was at work at KNWA.

In the next few months, I would learn how much my family loved me, what the word *friendship* means, and what it meant to set yourself free. I would also continue on toward what I call "my path."

I am a firm believer that God puts people in our lives at just the right moment—people who can somehow help blurry vision become clear. Case in point: Naomi Judd was in town, speaking at a few local events. I got to be the local emcee. Before one of the shows, for lack of a better word, I was in the bathroom crying. The days before had been rough with Richard, and I was nearing the end of my strength. I wanted to do my job, but I needed a few minutes to clear my head. I had just cleaned up my face when Naomi walked by me as she left a bathroom stall. She wouldn't know me and probably wouldn't remember the girl crying the bathroom. But I won't forget what she said: "I don't know what it is, but remember you have to take care of you, honey." I was blown away.

Immediately following that program, I went to see my Uncle Stacy Jones at work. I needed to talk with someone I could trust, and he too was there for me. I knew this kind of pain was going to be unbearable for my father, and I needed a little guidance. I won't go into that conversation except to say, "Thank you, Uncle Stacy, for listening."

Sometimes a daughter can't talk to her father because she knows her pain will only cause him even more pain. Having Uncle Stacy helped me get my head together. It was almost as if he opened the door for me to find a safe place. I didn't tell him everything; just that I was unhappy, and that I was scared. Looking back, it was the start of me developing a plan. That plan was slowly in the works, starting with the day I asked myself a very important question: How did I get here? I know everyone's answer is different.

For me, changes happened slowly. At first, those changes were subtle; later they were defined and precise. The world I was living in went from comments said in anger by a man who said he loved me to a man walking toward me with his hands headed toward a firm grasp around my neck and throat.

In my time with Richard, it was as though he knew I would adjust my baseline for "normal" if he didn't chip away too quickly. I mean, it started with normal complaints anyone might have about me or anyone else. Human complaints. We all have our strengths and weaknesses.

Eventually, there were strange mind games: "Do you really think those girls like you? They aren't your friends.

They hate you." Later, it got worse: "If you go to work, I'll slit your dog's throat," and eventually, "I don't feel anything and wouldn't even care if you died."

For me, that was the hardest part. Some of those things are just too hard to remember. The emotional abuse seemed much harder than the physical. I say that, knowing that anytime you are hit it does hurt emotionally as well. However, you can watch a bruise heal, and somehow, as the discolored skin returns to normal, it offers you hope. When it goes away, you think your relationship is getting better. You can see it get better, with a mental abrasion that's not necessarily true. The mind can take years to heal.

By the time I understood what was happening, it was almost too late. I had spent so much time trying to make things better that I forgot what I needed. I lost myself in an unhealthy relationship that was sucking the life out of me daily. The worst part: I'd gotten so good at hiding marks or covering situations or overcompensating, I thought no one else knew. I later learned I was wrong. What became clear was that I couldn't survive this much longer. Already my grandparents were calling my parents in Tulsa. After I left the relationship, my mom told me about those calls. She said my grandmothers were asking if I was okay. Both said my eyes looked sad on the news. They told her they were worried about me. My sweet family. They wanted to help. All I had to do was let them.

Where Do I Go from Here?

Again, I think this is another answer that will be a little different for everyone. I do think at least two factors are a must: God and help. I began to work on my relationship at the same time I was working to rebuild myself. I didn't really understand that until much later.

I called a friend one night and asked him to meet me at a nearby McDonald's. Richard and I had just finished one of our worst fights. There were holes in the walls, I knew I was going to have bruises on my body, I was shaking and afraid because again I knew this call was a cry for help. Richard was watching me make the call, screaming at me right up until my friend answered the phone. I was too afraid to call 911, and Richard knew the reasons. I knew those calls were often published in the local paper. I was already embarrassed by our situation. Why would I want someone to read our issues in the paper especially when I wasn't in a safe place? I regret that moment. I shouldn't have been ashamed to ask for help. Looking back, I wish I had called the police. But I was worried about embarrassing my family. I was worried about losing my job and not having a way to support myself. I just wanted it to all go away. Every day was a matter of walking on eggshells and would it be a good week or a bad week. My friend eventually called me back and asked where I was. I had to tell that person I couldn't come and that I would explain tomorrow and then hung up. I was afraid to leave my dog behind. I knew my friend couldn't take both of us in.

The fight stopped, in a manner I'm not ready to share because I hate remembering that night. But I can say I was safe for the moment. In the back of my mind I was going through all my options. I knew what Richard had threatened to do to my pet. As strange as that sounds, I couldn't leave behind the animal that had helped me through so much. He was my comfort and at times, my protector. When I would lock myself in a room for protection, I'd take my dog with me. I felt better when he was by my side, as though he wouldn't be hurt and neither would I.

Counselor

Richard would often not speak to me for days after fights. It was a hostile environment. I was afraid to speak. The silence was thick, deafening, and scary. You could feel the anger from both of us. I was more nervous during those times than any other.

It would have to be his idea to make up. Somehow this time I got him to sit down with me. We both admitted to faults and things we could do better. I found a Christian, licensed counselor. I started to go to therapy sessions. I found a safe haven and a place where I could get help without judgment. I asked Richard if he would go with me. I even told him to call the counselor and talk with him. I wanted Richard to have the right to choose someone different if he wasn't comfortable. I knew if Richard didn't feel comfortable, the sessions wouldn't do any good.

I eventually got Richard to go with me. Richard wanted to work on things. We both did. We both had fears. Looking at yourself is the hardest thing to do. I must say, I think somewhere inside of him he must have had intentions to try. He had a lot of valid points about me and us. This was a hard time for me because I wanted to believe we would be able to get better together.

But I noticed something soon into our visits. These sessions were more like a game for him. Or at least that's how I felt. He wanted to "win." Richard didn't care about what he had done or even what I had done. He didn't want to look at marks on my body or talk about holes in the wall. He wanted to be in power and keep score. I quickly learned that counseling only works if you are *both* honest and *both* try. I felt that our counseling sessions only delayed Richard, meaning he would try for a few days, maybe even a week, and then we would quickly spiral downward. Sometimes he would even conveniently forget things. One time he looked at our therapist and explained how our fights didn't include violence anymore. I'm not sure what possessed me, but I spoke up and said, "Richard, you got mad at me and broke the lights in the garage and then spread them over the hood of the car and the floor so I would step in the glass." I went to the bathroom and noticed the glass and asked him if a light bulb had broken, and he let me know he broke the bulbs and placed the glass. That was a big deal for several reasons, not the least of which included the fact that I was wearing a walking cast. If I'd stepped in glass, I would have been helpless and slower to move away. I knew that. On some level, so did Richard.

Our relationship was an unhealthy roller coaster, and I no longer found the highs worth the lows. I could see what was happening and felt helpless. I finally figured out that in a relationship, both people have to work on the weaknesses. I couldn't do it all. In fact, the counselor eventually told me I tried to take too much responsibility for all that went wrong. The longer we remained in counseling, the more I began to see my life as it truly was: non-existent. I had learned to ignore my inner voice, my gut instinct. I was lost. All my time was consumed by keeping this terrible secret and trying to keep the peace at home.

We were having a "good week" at one point when we headed out of town for a family fishing trip. I thought it might offer us a nice break from our normal environment. Everything was going okay until my family started to notice how Richard talked to me when he thought no one could hear or was listening. How he even shoved me out of his way, and how he shut my arm in the bathroom door when I didn't move out of his way quickly enough. But it was the night he decided to show his rear that the family became more aware that what perhaps they all suspected was happening behind closed doors.

The last night of our family trip, Richard went to bed early. We were all laughing and having a good time. So my father asked if he should go tease Richard and wake him up with the video camera. Understand, my father was trying to be funny. My sister, brother-in-law, mother, and niece were all still up, playing and watching television in the cabin.

McKenna Raley, Neile Jones-Batie, Leah Raley
Photo by Lori Staedke

I thought Richard was in an okay place, so I told my dad to go ahead. I knew he wanted to tease Richard like he would his own kids. Soon after, my dad came out of the room where Richard was with the strangest look on his face, and he didn't really say anything. Then Richard came out screaming and grabbing himself (in front of my three-year-old niece and the rest of the family) and turned to my father, saying things no child should hear. Everyone was in shock. My sister said, "Did he just say what I think he did?"

I froze. Later, when Richard went to bed, my mother told me she knew at that point that something was going on. She knew I needed help, but she wasn't sure how to move forward because she knew it was a delicate situation. All she wanted was her baby safe. She said I pulled my knees to my chest and seemed to go into a daze. In all of this, somehow my niece didn't hear exactly what Richard said. But she was there. My life flashed before my eyes, and I just kept thinking, *Oh my gosh. What if he stole some of her innocence? I am responsible for introducing him to my family. I'm the one who said, "Hey, this guy's all right." This child is a product of my sister and her husband's love.* If I brought someone into the family who would harm her by scaring her, even if his anger was directed at someone else, I couldn't live with that.

It's strange that the instinct to protect someone else helped me decide to protect myself. I could never forgive myself if she was hurt. Then it dawned on me. Richard no longer cared what he did or whom he did it in front of. He had no remorse and never would. He felt perfectly secure in his actions.

The next morning I got up early. Like when I was a child, I met my father with a rod and reel down by the river. He was so sweet and kind. I'll never forget that conversation. He stood there with his fly rod, and I stood with him. It's a moment I'll never forget—the candid honesty and concern between a father and a daughter, a father's love and apology for something that was in no way his fault, and the way he let me know the family wanted to help. He let me know the choices were all mine. He also let me know it was taking everything in him not to handle Richard himself, but in the end, Dad knew that wouldn't empower me any and it would only hurt all of us. Before the talk ended, Dad made it clear: all I had to do was let them know how and when. I felt nothing but love. And I heard him loud and clear. I just cried big alligator, slow, Arkansas tears. It would soon be time to pack up and leave. And soon everything would come to a head. I ended up leaving that trip so saddened and afraid, but also with a renewed strength. I knew I had the support of my family. I knew they would help me, and I knew all I had to do was figure out a way to get free of the emotional blockage that kept me caged in fear. Looking back, I know this was a dangerous time for me because Richard could see I was starting to get a little stronger again. He also knew for the first time in a long while the people around me had been able to make me feel safe, and that gave me a little sense of who I used to be. Looking back, I know it scared him. He started trying to squeeze every ounce of that out of me on the car ride home. That ride—the words, the things he did—are still some of my worst memories. The whole way home I kept hearing my father's voice, my mother's, my sister's. I knew the time was coming. I knew I had to leave. I knew I was going to leave. No matter how much hurt he tried to inflict, he couldn't steal my hope. He couldn't make my family stop loving me. I needed to know that, and somehow Richard, without meaning to, helped make that knowledge appear by giving my family a chance to catch a glimpse, a flicker of what life was like living with him. They saw; they acted; I was mentally getting my plans together.

The following week I headed back to work. Family vacation was over, and I was trying to make Richard think we were fine. I knew if I could distract him by acting like all the rejuvenation I'd found wasn't real, I'd find a way to escape. I came home from work, but Richard was still not talking to me. He was more than mad. He had been drinking, which never helped anything. It meant another night of walking on eggshells, hoping nothing in his emotional arsenal cracked. A crack would mean a huge fight and danger. I remember he was grilling outside. I so desperately wanted to find some peace with him, so I asked him if we were ever going to speak or be a normal couple. I, of course, started crying, and because I just had nothing left—I was empty emotionally and exhausted from the intense mental drain of limbo; the limbo of wanting to leave but not quite being able to; of wanting to make it work and knowing it never would; trying to leave and wishing that staying would somehow repair the colossal damage that had been done. Despite a calm attempt to find neutral ground, the yelling started. I am sure I didn't help ease the tension because I was tired of taking the brunt of everything Richard had to offer—verbal poison that could make even the strongest person drained by the anticipation of what mental or physical blow would come next. Then Richard headed toward me, yelling, "You are right! I was wrong, and I know it!" It was as though he was fighting himself, but I was the source he could find to blame for the realization of what he had become. At the same time, it was as if he couldn't see me. He could only see someone or something he needed to hate. I backed up and yelled quickly, "I don't want to be right! I don't have to be right!" Richard said, "But you are right." I kept backing up, and he came toward me with his hands headed for my throat as if to mimic strangling me. In all the fights we'd had, his hands had never approached my throat before, not like this. A light went on in my head, and I knew. I knew to be quiet and get into a different room. I knew to lock the door, to get Phong in the same room with me. I did. I sat still in the darkness, watching Richard's shadow pass back and forth across the light coming from the bottom of the door. I held Phong still and I stayed still just waiting, watching, and praying for Richard to finally fall asleep or pass out.

I didn't sleep that night. The sad part is, this wasn't the worst of our fights. I just cried quietly, pet Phong, and prayed and focused on what I knew was coming. I knew what I had to face, what I had let happen. I was at work the next day, as was Richard. We'd been fighting all day via the telephone. After numerous phone calls back and forth, I knew this relationship had to end. I think he knew I was trying to end things, and every time I'd try to calmly move in that direction, he'd hang up on me. It was like a game for him, almost as if he wanted to be able to say, "See; look, she kept calling me," a charade he needed to put on for himself when inside he knew I was about to say good-bye. Finally I called him and asked him three questions, including, "Do you love me?" He said no. I even asked if we could go to the counselor one last time so things could end amicably. In no uncertain terms, he said no. I told him good-bye and wished him well. I made the decision to not ever speak directly to him once I'd said my piece. I wanted to keep my strength and not allow him any opportunity to bring me yet another fake apology.

I remember He laughed as we hung up. It was the last time I ever had to hear that sarcastic, mean, cruel laugh. I can't explain the calmness that came over me in that moment. It was as if a higher power was guiding me. Everything seemed so surreal. I hung up the phone and finished my work. I eventually left the television station and headed to lunch with three close friends. I told them what happened and what had been happening for a long time. I then sat in a local restaurant with them and cried. I knew I was about to fall apart because I felt safe again to do so. And I did. I headed to the counselor, knowing how hard that visit would be. I told him what happened. He then said something I'll never forget: "Neile, you can never be alone with him again." Now think about that reality. I asked for clarity, and I got it. I knew the answers, but I also knew I needed to hear someone else say them.

After our session, I went back up to my office and found a man I knew I could trust, my supervisor. I explained to him that I needed some time off to get myself out of my situation. He hugged me and told me I could have whatever time I needed. I left the office, got my dog, my checkbook, and the things I needed, and headed to Tulsa to my parents.

The hour-and-a-half drive is a daze. My mind was all over the place. I was a mix of emotions, and I just wanted to see my parents. I wanted my sister. I wanted the comfort of those who loved me. I wanted to say I was sorry. I wanted to explain everything. I was so scared of what I'd allowed to happen. I was so disappointed in myself that I couldn't make the relationship work. That night I sat my mother and father down and said, "I have to tell you everything that's happened so I don't continue to make excuses, so I don't continue to lie. So I don't go back."

I knew that if I took them through the whole gory thing—every nasty fight, my mistakes and behavior, as well as his—I would be able to gain my strength and some sense of self-respect. I had to go back and explain every time someone had asked about a bruise and I'd come up with something other than what really happened. The three of us sat at the kitchen table and cried. It was like a cleansing, as though I could finally stop protecting someone who had absolutely no interest in protecting me. I know that sounds strange, but it's true. I can't explain why I felt so loyal to someone who had no loyalty to anything but power. I watched both my parents' eyes well up with tears, and both of them grieved for my pain and suffering. The hard part was I knew that they both blamed themselves for what had happened. It wasn't my parents' fault. It was our fault, Richard and Neile's fault. When I was done, both my parents hugged me and told me it was going to be okay. That moment that was the safest I'd felt in what seemed like forever. I sat on the couch and mentally crashed. They told me we would get through this together. And we did. We made a plan quickly. What I later learned, family and friends started calling my parents, saying, "How can we help? What can we do? When do you need us?" They never asked me anything that would make me hurt. They just moved with me as I tried to find footing and freedom from a pain that even they couldn't fully understand.

I will never be able to take away the hurt I caused them by bringing this person around them. I can do my best to never let it happen again. I felt so relieved, but at the same time so saddened by all the time I'd wasted and the pain I'd caused my family. I misjudged a person's character, and they had to pay the price for that with me. At least, that's how I felt. Perhaps my sister put it best when she told my dad, "It's time to circle the wagons."

I think I sat on my parents' couch for two days before my mother finally convinced me to take a bath. I would venture to guess I was in shock—shock that I finally chose to speak up, that I left, and that I was going to be okay. I knew my family was about to go through hell and back with me. I also had a renewed since of self, probably because they left all the decisions up to me.

After that day, I moved in with some friends and never told anyone where I was staying. I didn't want Richard to come after this couple or me. And I didn't want anyone to feel pressure to lie to protect me. I was done with that. I would take different routes to work and leave Phong at different friends' houses. It was great for him because it gave him a play date. It was a hard, lonely time. I felt homeless, as if I was just floating from one friend's house to another. I kept working and tried to keep my chin up. I would go home and just go to bed. I didn't want to talk to anyone. I didn't want to hurt others anymore. I had no strength to open up to people. I had no patience for new friends. I had a broken heart and was in mourning for the person I used to be. At the same time, I was getting letters and e-mails from Richard about how much he loved me. He was mailing letters to family members as if to tie up any loose ends. We just put the letters in a box. The words were what they had always been: untrue.

I was living in a prison I had to learn to escape from. I wasn't able to be much of friend because I felt I had nothing to give. I felt betrayed and confused. I was trying to learn to trust my judgment again. The worst part was I was part of the whole betrayal because I failed myself. In the nights, I remember missing Richard. It didn't take long for me to realize I didn't miss the real Richard. I missed the fake Mr. Charming that I knew when we first started dating. Soon I could see what a blessing it was for me to escape that time. Looking back, I was so blessed. I had a place to go. I had family and friends I could turn to for help. I can't tell you the number of people who reached out to me and helped me pick myself up. People I will always love and never forget. My mother and father knew exactly what to say and do. I just can't explain how wonderful my parents and sister and brother-in-law and friends were. My parents had the strength to let me find a comfortable silence again. They also knew that when it came to decisions, those choices had to be mine. They could give me advice and insight, but in the end they knew by letting me make my own decisions, I was being empowered again. They let me bring Phong everywhere. They knew how much he meant to me during those terrible times, and they weren't about to ask me to leave him anywhere I wasn't going to be. They loved each other and I think became more conscious of how important it was for me to be around healthy relationships. Most importantly, every time I had a thought about something I'd done wrong, they listened and didn't try to nullify my feelings. They just kept saying, "Neile, you did what you had to do," and "Neile, none of this was your fault."

And my sister, Holly, will always be my best friend. She helped me so much along the way, knowing when to laugh, knowing when to make me move on, and all the while not coddling me too much. I can't say enough about my family and friends. From my folks to my aunts, uncles, and cousins, they were in many ways the only reflection of the Neile Jones I once knew. They could see me even when I couldn't, when the reflection didn't match what I thought I was supposed to see. One friend, Kari, even flew me to her home in California. She knew I couldn't afford the ticket, but she also knew I needed to see her and her husband. I remember when I went there, she told me to do what I needed to do. So I spent the days looking at the mountains and hiking one near her condo. Every day I would get a little higher up and closer to the top. Every step brought deep thoughts and soul searching. At night she and I spent time talking about old times and anything and everything. She was doing what I needed. She was giving me a safe place to accept me, to accept that I, like everyone, have flaws and I am also a human being who deserves happiness and laughter and dreams. In Dallas, my friend Tina gave me another stop that allowed me to gather strength. We spent time talking and visiting about everything old times and new. These two ladies helped me laugh and remember that it's okay to be who I am and that I don't need to try to fit the mold anyone has created for me.

The Work Is Just Beginning

When you leave, there are many hard nights. The first few in Tulsa with my parents were hard. I finally let down from the façade I'd been living. I was so grateful to have parents who were understanding and supportive and not judgmental. Those first few hours of confusion seem like the hardest, but in all actuality, they were the easiest. You will find that the noise you hear in the silence of an empty room can be unlike any other obstacle. It's those moments when you are alone with you and what you've become that you first start to realize how much work you have ahead of you. You have so many questions: What have I become? What did I do wrong? Why did I do that? Why didn't I leave sooner?

During this time, I became more and more aware that a part of me died when I left that relationship—the part of me he molded into shape, knowing he could slowly chip away at my belief in me. Like a warped artist with fresh clay. For example, I said "I'm sorry" all the time. You couldn't talk to me for more than ten minutes before the words came flying out of my mouth. The sad part? I didn't notice until someone else drew the issue to my attention. Two things seemed to help me and they might just help someone else, too.

One: write in a journal.

> By Wed. am my cell phone was turned off (by you) and our aol password changed. You told Chris M. I'd just gone someplace to cool off. Friday I came and took my things the worst/hardest day of my life...and my family suffered too. Now I can honestly say I am happier. I never have to be hit with a broom or be called a ██████. I never have to hide marks on my body or lie to my family about why you are acting strange.
>
> I am free now and God willing I will never lose myself trying to save someone else... again.

Two: change your type.

The Journal

One of the most helpful recommendations for me was to journal.

Sometimes I would write down things I knew I couldn't

ever say to Richard. When I left, I left. There would be no going back. Yes, that was good. But it also meant finding answers by myself and learning to let go of things I had no control over.

I still go back and look at my words. I was full of raw emotion—fear, anxiety, anger, and pain. I wrote about praying for him to go to anger management. I wrote about how if he could just ... if he would just ...

I would suggest these things to anyone working through a tough choice.

1. Pray in your journal.

My conversations with God on paper were just as fulfilling as my internal and verbal prayers. I prayed to understand God's will. I would ask for forgiveness, and I would ask God to help me forgive my plethora of mistakes. I asked God to help me forgive myself and Richard. I wasn't asking God to help me forget. I wasn't asking God to help me go back to a relationship that had been so unhealthy. I was asking for a way to help my heart heal. I knew for a complete self-awareness I had to deal with my anger and disappointments, which meant I had to get to a point where I no longer harbored anger and resentment. I became comfortable alone with my thoughts. I became unafraid to face the things that got me in such a dark place. The combination of writing these prayers down and articulating them gave me the power to see, feel, remember, hear, and work through things that maybe before the journal were too hard.

2. Write down your biggest fears.

I had so many fears. I was worried about talking with friends and family. What do you say? How much is too much? How do you explain all you endured without telling people more than anyone should have to hear? I also used this area of my thoughts as a place to think about things I wanted to work through with my counselor.

I wrote down a fear of being alone. I wrote about my fears of seeing Richard face-to-face again. One of my biggest concerns centered on happiness. Did I deserve happiness? Why? Why did I keep choosing people who weren't good for me? I mean, I picked Richard. I stayed with Richard. I knew I had to work through that reality. This is hard, but it's also a great exercise for dealing with the things that trouble you the most. Fear can be our greatest downfall. If we don't face our fear or, as my dad says, "get back up on that horse," we may never find true courage. For me, getting back up on the horse was all about facing my fears.

> We went back to our family vacation spot in June. Much different than the last time. I was a little worried the trip would hurt and or be bitter sweet. Instead it was beautiful. We finished and ate dinner. The girls swam with Holly and Kevin. We walked the little park with the peacocks and then hung out. There was even a wedding...funny thing it made me even more hopeful for the future, for life... love.

3. Dreams

Part of an abusive and controlling situation is the loss of control. I tried to remember things I wanted for myself. I wanted to feel strong again, both inside and out. I wanted to remember all that used to be me. I had forgotten my sense of self. I learned that by thinking about my beliefs and dreams, I could rediscover me. I could remember what was important to me. I also wanted to find my happiness. I wanted to look in the mirror and like what I saw in the reflection. I know it sounds corny, but you stop looking. You don't even know it consciously, but one day you realize that for however long, you've spent the majority of your time working to please someone else. That may mean you've worked to please those around you, keeping your secret. It may mean you've given up any opinion you once had for a superficial peace, a peace that never really existed but you still try to find. My dream included real peace, an internal realization of me and God's true unconditional love for me. I wanted to redefine myself. My dreams included everything from being physically fit to self-assured and independent. Those were dreams that I would accomplish, but I knew it would be a long, hard road. I was ready for that challenge. Writing down my dreams gave me something else positive to focus on for a happier life. It's up to you to reclaim that part of yourself. I'm not talking about going in and taking "things" as in objects. I'm talking about finding the ability to believe in what maybe you had forgotten. These words on paper were the start of me taking back what was mine all along.

It's getting easier everyday and everyday I get stronger and work to take care of myself a little more. I go back and forth between being a little scared and a little excited. Excited that there's a whole new life out there for me to believe in. I know there's something better a head for me and my life. A happiness I've yet to experience. I know change is here to stay and I know I'm going to be okay.

4. Write down the bad.

Now, I'm not telling you this because I want you to focus on the bad. I am saying to write down the worst of the worst. There are several reasons for this. Sometimes if we retrace our steps, we can see what we missed the first time—warning signs that might help us learn so we don't make the same mistakes again. Another very important thing to remember is when you leave someone like Richard, he will fight to get you back. That person will say and do all the "right things," hoping to entangle you back in his web. By writing down the bad, you are giving yourself a place to revisit what you must remember. Not a place to stay angry, but a place to revisit and remind yourself of the pattern that person follows. I could see the pattern more clearly when it was on paper. A person working to get you back in his or her control can say or do or pretend to be anything that person thinks you want to hear or want him to be. They prey on your forgiving heart.

For me, the key has been to forgive and not forget. The reason I can't let myself forget is because forgetting would eliminate any lesson I learned.

I have found that the bad pages can be the hardest and the most helpful. Writing down scary times can also lead to healing. Sometimes you can face things on paper slowly and gain an insight that's been previously unattainable. It can also help open your eyes to unhealthy patterns in a relationship—extreme ups and downs that surpass any roller coaster you've ever bought a ticket to ride. I had to write down the bad so when Richard started sending me letters and e-mails, I could remind myself of the pattern. This was just him doing the same old thing. Nothing new. I could see the trend and remind myself of the full personality that came along with Richard. It allowed me to see the pattern in a way that would help me avoid becoming part of that pattern again.

5.   Write about how life is different.

I used to write about how thankful I was my dog was safe. I know that sounds strange, but Richard was cruel to my dog because he knew it hurt me. I felt so guilty about that. Then I felt good about protecting my dog and giving us both a better life. I wrote about my days and how any scrapes or marks on my body had nothing to do with violence. I knew if I had a bruise, I'd been clumsy and run into a corner somewhere. I remember looking at a mark on my shoulder from a cabinet. It actually made me smile because it wasn't something I'd gotten in a moment when I was trying to defend myself. It was something that just happened. I also wrote about how good it was to actually tell someone exactly what had happened, knowing I didn't have to cover anything up to protect myself from retaliation at home later. And because I'd been given an opportunity to say "I'm sorry." What I could see was anytime I was hurting, my family and friends hurt for me too.

Life was anything I wanted it to be (still is). I picked a Bible study and started walking outside with friends. I took day trips to the lake or went hiking with my dog. I was spreading my wings again. I could write on paper about every little thing that made me happy. I had no worries about boring someone else or pleasing someone else. After all, this was about me. Not in a selfish, totally absorbed way, but in a healing-process way. Writing down what made me happy helped me discover what I liked—not what I liked because someone else thought I should like; what truly gave me pleasure about the world and learning to appreciate that it's okay to have likes and dislikes.

6. Write down your blessings and what you are thankful for, every day.

I found that this section started to grow in my journal. It would eventually become the longest section. I learned to be grateful and thankful for every moment that led to the next—the good and the bad. I began to appreciate my true friends. My family became even more important. Things I once took for granted became embedded in my mind. I always appreciated my grandparents, but I remember going to see them not too long after I left Richard. Grandma and Grandpa Klober were in their backyard peeling and canning pears. I remember the way the sun felt on my face and how strong my grandpa's hands looked, how they were honest hands, strong but gentle, as if time had given them a lifetime of garden lessons. I loved to watch my grandparents together and how they loved each other. My appreciation for their relationship helped me understand more about what I wanted for my life. I remember sitting in the hospital with my granddaddy Jones during his final days on earth. I thought to myself about his love for my granny and how the two of them had so much fun together and the love they shared. I was and am so thankful for them. In my life I was blessed to not only be a granddaughter but to have grandparents that were my friends. They, like my parents, taught me a lot. Their love for our family was a true blessing. Looking back on those blessings helped me see things much more clearly. My thank-you notes in my journal helped me to remember the littlest things that made a huge impact. I wrote about my friend Lisa who would send me cards for no reason. Each day I would look forward to the mail and a note about her and her family. It made me realize how we can all help others even with seemingly the smallest acts of kindness.

7.   A checklist

Okay, first let me advise you to take at least a year off from any real dating. Take the time to figure out what got you into an unsafe situation. If you figure out where you came from, you're more likely to figure out where you are going. What were the significant relationships in your life like? Did you always choose men who fit the classic "bad boy" description? If so, what did that mean? And why did you choose them? How do you figure out a way to choose people who will be a better fit and nicer human beings as a whole? I also suggest the time off because your emotions are going to be all over the place long before you are grounded again. If you date, you'll probably end up hurting someone because you'll end up in a rebound relationship. You may also falsely attach to another person and displace your feelings from the previous relationship. Time off can be the best way to learn from your mistakes. At least, that's what I found with the help from those around me. I remember wanting to date someone really bad for me. But a very strong friend told me what I needed to hear, not what I *wanted* to hear, but what I *needed*.

Now, that brings me to the list. After a year or so goes by and you've started to figure out yourself, then you probably will start to think about what you want in a partner.

1. Christian

2. A man able to laugh at himself

3. Someone who helps me laugh at myself

4. My best friend

5. Someone to support me and who will let me support him

6. A man who has a strong family connection and who is respectful

But you can also write things like:

1. A man able to sustain a job
2. Someone to appreciate my career
3. A dog lover
4. Someone who is romantic
5. A person who likes working out
6. A man with good table manners

8. Spend time with people in healthy relationships.

I wanted to be around my sister and her family all the time. My friend Chris had just met the most wonderful woman I knew he would marry. I wanted to be around Chris and Kim to remind myself that those types of relationships existed. Kim quickly became a wonderful new friend who was very understanding about everything I'd been through. The two of them gave me fun opportunities to hang out and not feel like someone who had just survived a horrible life experience. They just loved me without making me feel ashamed of anything I'd just been through. I spent time with my parents and my dear friends from childhood, people who would protect me from my past without hindering the process of me finding my way back to my path. I called a friend's mom and took her to lunch because I had a feeling we had something in common. She was wonderful (thank you, Sally). I sought out people I'd been distant from and tried to reconnect with people I'd been hiding from.

Change Your Type

Your so-called "type" got you into probably one of the worst relationships you've had, so what were all the other people in your life like? Did you date others who cheated, told you what to do, or brought out the worst in you?

How did you meet those people?

Why not try meeting people through friends? Or spend more time getting involved in new activities just because you want to and not because the weekly meeting could mean a chance for some fresh meat? I think a lot of people spend so much time looking for "the one" that they don't realize "the one" might be right in front of them. The problem could be the search itself.

What exactly has been so great about the people you've known? Okay, you've probably been physically attracted to the person. In fact, in the beginning, you may have been "swept off your feet," but what else? How much depth did the person have? Did you think about a future and a 50/50 relationship?

The guy who freaks out when another man talks to you or seems to get jealous over nothing is probably not the guy for you.

I looked back at my pattern and my old "type." The nice guys didn't last with me.

That was my fault. I kept picking men who would say and do anything all in an effort to tell me what I wanted to hear.

One day when you're sold on the idea that he's "the

one," the flip flop act begins. Either my job was the problem or I was too fat or I needed to stay in the relationship because no one else would want me. Or I didn't want to fail at the relationship when in fact staying in the relationship was actually a greater failure because I would have learned much sooner from my mistakes by leaving. I discovered that being afraid of failure was the biggest failure of all.

The other thing I discovered was that I picked, in the words of my father, stray dogs. You know, the guys who seem rejected at every turn and just need someone to take them in and love them. Okay, let me tell you wonderful women out there with the wonderful ability to nurture: men and stray dogs aren't the same. A canine is less likely to bite you than a man pretending he has issues you can repair. Just remember that the stray dog act is just that: an act.

Changing my "type" meant finding someone who loved me and all of my scars—not a man to feel sorry for me, not a man to rescue me, not a man to fix me. It also meant finding a man who was whole without me. We all love the line "You complete me," from the movie *Jerry Maguire*, and yes, I believe that's a true emotion. But before you can offer anyone anything, you have to complete yourself. Be whole on your own and find someone else who is in the same boat. We spend too much time trying to fill an empty place in our hearts with a boyfriend. We need to dig into that empty place ourselves. With God's help, you'll fill the gap.

I needed a man who could accept me, a man who would talk to me about politics, religion, friends, sex, love, world peace, anything and everything, just to know my thoughts;

a man who would express his thoughts on the same issues and help me gain knowledge in a whole new capacity. I wanted a man who could express the good and the bad without a lack of respect. I needed someone with confidence and humility. Yes, a person can have both. Think about your old "type" and discover your new "type." When you are ready to date again, you'll find that this process goes on for a while. You'll probably also soon discover that you're not so concerned about a boyfriend or husband. You're more concerned about discovering you and trying new things.

Make a list of dreams. I am a firm believer that when you write something down, you are more likely to achieve that goal. If you want to find happiness, you will. If you want to work on yourself, you can. If you want to get a better job, you'll find it. What you have to do is deprogram yourself. If you've been in an abusive relationship, you've been broken down in more ways than one. You've done and said things you never thought were possible. You made choices. Now, before you give me the eye roll, hear me out. In life, everyone makes choices, good and bad. Why? Because no human being is perfect. Somewhere along the line you'll have to face what decisions you made that were good and right and what ones were incredibly wrong. Now, what this also means is taking the right amount of responsibility for where you are in life. You have to choose to find yourself. You have to choose to want more for yourself, your family, and your life. Now this next one you might have a hard time with, but give it time. Okay, brace yourself. Are you ready? You can choose not to be a victim anymore.

Learning to Love Again

I had numerous people tell me to take time off from dating. I was told not to jump in to anything for a while. I made mistakes until I finally understood you can't replace emptiness with an empty relationship. It's my belief that until you know who you are and what you want, you can't offer much to anyone one else. At one point, I just decided not to date. I needed to focus on finding me. That meant looking at me in a way I'd never done before. I spent time in Bible study and in counseling alone. I learned to be comfortable in a quiet room. In my relationship with Richard, I had become so conditioned to believe silence was uncomfortable, I felt I had to talk almost all the time. Silence in my past had been a warning sign that Richard was about to explode. Silence can be a good thing, and that was a big hurdle for me, but once I passed it, I didn't look back. Then I went through a phase where I only wanted to be alone. I didn't want anyone to ask me how I was doing because I didn't want to lie. And I didn't want to say out loud again, "I'm in a lot of pain." As time moved on, I began to see and understand that I'm not any different from anyone else. I'm a human being who makes mistakes. It became easier for me to open up to people because I'd opened up to myself. I soon found my "gut check" again and made myself a promise to never ignore that internal alarm. It's something I stick with today. Each one of these things made me stronger, more independent, happy with being alone, happy being with friends. I finally got a place of my own and started having fun. I decorated it how I wanted. I went to church a lot during this time. I would often secretly drive to Tulsa and sit in the chapel where I'd grown up. I spent one of my best Christmas Eves at the Methodist Church on Dickson Street in Fayetteville.

My first Christmas Eve alone was spent in this church. It might have been the hardest Christmas Eve of my life, but it was like a cleansing in a way. I went to the service alone that night. I found a seat near the back where I could hear and be surrounded by the songs I'd grown up with as a child. The sermon this night seemed tailor-made for someone like me. I listened as if no one else was in the room and hung on to every word the Pastor said. I had been pulled into a moment that changed my heart.

As the sermon wrapped up, the lights dimmed and Communion started. I was praying over and over and over, *God, please forgive me. Please forgive me for any pain I have caused my family for every lie; for every bruise I hid; for every time I felt sorry for myself and forgot that all I needed to do was listen to you. I am so sorry I forgot my strength. Help me find it again. Show me the way. Help me heal, God.*

My prayers soon turned to thank-you as I began to see that all along the way, God gave me everything I needed to take care of myself. *I am one of his creatures. He loves me unconditionally. My true friends and family love me. I have to love myself. If I don't love myself, I can't expect to share love with anyone else.* All of these powerful thoughts were moving through my heart and mind.

Soon the candles were lit. The congregation began to sing songs most of us have known since we were children. It was in this moment that I could almost feel a warm hug around me. I could feel warmth in my heart. I sang every word I could as I wept. I cried for the person I had become and the girl I was finally letting go of so I could become the woman I've always been. It was as if I'd been given permission to mourn the loss of everything I knew and of everything that had happened that no one knew. My tears became full of just that: joy. I knew I had found a place in my heart that felt familiar. I had found the Neile I knew before Richard. I am sure the people around me probably wondered what was wrong, but I didn't care. That night, the church allowed me to soul search and begin to find peace again. I left that night and ended up on the Fayetteville Square before the holiday season had completely passed. I could finally see the colors in the lights again. I could hear the tunes of my heart. I could feel the comfort of a reckoning with myself. I would often get to the square in the early morning around midnight or one. I would just sit with Phong and look at him as he sat there, knowing that neither of us would ever endure such events again. I found my light. I found my self-respect.

Time would pass quickly now, and so would the seasons. Interestingly enough, the most difficult time in my life now is a time that I look back upon with fondness. I think because it got me to a place where I was comfortable in my own skin and I knew everything else was just an accessory.

A friend I called MaMa Levine died suddenly during this time. She was a woman who looked after me in a way that my own mother would be proud of. I went to the visitation for her funeral. That night, a friend who had twins was with me. Both boys got away from her, so I ran after one, and before I knew it, another man had the other boy in his arms. As I walked toward him, he smiled and said, "Looks like we have a matched pair." His kind eyes sparkled, as he seemed to be very proud of his quick thoughts. But I wasn't ready to believe in nice guys again yet, so I just handed him the other child and said something like, "Umm, yeah." I knew he'd have his hands full, so I just walked off, making it clear I had no interest.

I think God was smiling upstairs because he was preparing me for a man who would become the love of my life. You see, my sister, Holly, back in Tulsa, was on a mission. She'd asked almost everyone whom she could set me up with or if they knew anyone. Holly wasn't alone in this quest. I reached a point where I just had to tell people I was not ready for anything serious. But finally one day it would be my sister, of course, who found my now husband. I got a call from her, and she said a friend had gone to high school with this guy named Greg Batie. Holly's friend called him and asked if he'd like to be fixed up. He said, and I quote, "I'm not ready to hang curtains or anything, but yeah." You see, Greg, like me, had been through his own heartache. We had both been through a divorce, neither of us proud of that in any way. On our first lunch meeting, we figured out we knew each other from the visitation where we met the year before. He was the nice guy who said, "Looks like we have a matched pair."

I was so hard on Greg. I mean, our first official date was for sure a challenge. Let me also say, before the night was over, we both agreed we were on our last first date— a feeling made possible by our ability to wait until the time was right for us to meet. We both had listened to our hearts, and we both believed God had a plan for us, a plan we didn't get in the way of. We are married now, and every day the relationship only seems to get better. It took a long time for me to be able to trust again. I told Greg about what had happened in what we call my "previous life." I told him so he would know I was truly trying to let him in. I wanted to be open with him about why I had become so guarded in my life. That was part of me opening up to him. I think it helped him understand how important it was and is for him to keep his word to me. Any glimpse of an untruth, and I wouldn't be around much. In a way that wasn't fair because I didn't give him room to make any mistakes. Over time, though, I was able to see that not every man is Richard. Not every man hits. Greg and I had our first disagreement, and it was hard. It was the first time a memory from the past was triggered, and I got scared of a person so gentle and kind. I mean, come on, he is human. But Greg isn't a violent person. He will defend those he loves, and he would never intentionally hurt them. That argument was such a big stepping stone for us and me. I would soon learn how to have healthy and fair disagreements. Sometimes I still laugh when we disagree because it's so easy to state my opinion and know I am safe. Greg's patience allows me to be who I am. He also showed me how a person can tell you the hardest things and not hurt you because they are telling you the truth out of love, not out of a need to be "right." He is my husband and my best friend. He opens the door for me not because he has to but because he wants to. It's just in him. I tell people Greg is a modern-day Jimmy Stewart gentleman to the bone. My sister told me once that the person you marry should have the best of every man you've ever known inside of him, meaning all those other people in your life were clues about what's to come. She was right. I see a piece of my dad, grandfathers, uncles, brothers-in-law—all good pieces wrapped up into one person

I believe God knew Greg would be able to show me how to trust again. And I thank God for this man and this love. I also thank God for Greg's family that is, of course, now my family. They have embraced me and loved me as their own.

Make a Difference

I try every day to make a difference for someone else's life. I don't mean that like I'm better than anyone else. I mean I know what it feels like to have a stranger be kind to you or a friend help you or hug you for no reason. I have learned that other women don't have the resources I had. Not all friends and family so quickly embrace a woman as she leaves a relationship that tore her apart.

I know many people who have dealt with a woman or man or child who keeps returning to an unhealthy relationship. That hurts their families, so the families feel forced to give up and move back, putting space between themselves and the bad situations. I understand that too. Some people in abusive relationships have no jobs, no education, or are married to someone very affluent and are afraid to leave. Male or female, I believe unless in self-defense, we don't need to hit each other. Homes should be peaceful places, not battlegrounds where the strong prey on loved ones trying to target their weaknesses to feel powerful.

One thing for me was knowing that people cared about me without judging me. I was doing enough of that on my own. I eventually began to work with a local shelter and the wonderful people who cared for others. I learned about an open-water swim to benefit the shelter, so I began to train. I had never been a swimmer like that, but I wanted to do something in honor of these families, so I swam a two-mile, open-water swim. It was a fundraiser for the shelter. I trained with people who were very kind and showed me so much respect and patience. I wanted to show someone else in a bad situation that getting out and being happy is possible. I knew that with every stroke I could help raise money, put to rest some of my demons, and maybe show a woman that someone who doesn't know her wants to help her see she deserves better. Women who were staying at one of the local shelters would often show up in the crowd to watch. The shelter advocates told me it means a lot to these ladies to see other people doing something to help, even if it's getting in a lake to swim a few miles and raise money for the place where they are staying.

Soon, I learned about a marathon. No, I'm not a runner. But I'm also not a quitter.

I knew I was going to finish this marathon if it took me all day.

Neile Jones–Batie crossing the finish line of
Hogeye Marathon in Fayetteville, Arkansas

And I finished. In fact, my friends rode their bikes beside me. My husband did the Hogeye Marathon on his bike. I had been up almost all night the night before. I knew I had to finish this 26.6-mile race for myself and for the women at the shelter. He knew the importance of that and the significance of that, so he and my friend Sarah LaVaute, along with a few others, got on their bikes or walked and jogged beside me the whole way.

Neile Jones-Batie and Sarah LaVaute

I had sent a letter to the shelter before the race, explaining how I believe leaving an abusive relationship can be like finishing a marathon. You have to do the work. You have to have a training plan. You will probably need help along the way, and that's why there are water stations set up. But if you just keep going, no matter how fast or how slow, you will reach the finish line.

When leaving an abusive relationship, you have to mentally train yourself for what's to come. You have to prepare, and you will more likely than not need some help along the way. But in the end, if you just keep going, if you don't give up and you keep your focus, you will find peace at the finish line.

In retrospect, it was a small act with a huge impact. You see, you don't always have to write a check. Sometimes you can send a long-distance hug. Later, I sent a copy of my bib to the shelter. I'm not sure, but I think it still hangs there today.

Some months are harder than others, but every month I try. It's a small thing to give someone a note that says, "Hey, I believe in you," or a hug that says, "Hey, I'm not judging you." Try it. Believe in someone you don't know. You'll find that that person and your act will teach you more about yourself.

I've included some pictures to share with you! Some are of friends and family. Some of dreams come true. All are pictures that include goals and achievements and people I've been able to meet because I chose to be free from my past. Had I stayed in that violent relationship, I don't believe I would have gotten to experience any of these great people and wonderful places. I've been able to emcee or speak at events that helped raise thousands of dollars and awareness for everything from diabetes research to breast cancer.

Neile Jones-Batie with husband, Greg Batie, at JDRF Gala; picture taken by Tom Ewart, NWA Photography

I have a husband who understands that a few hours on a Saturday night mean less money a charity has to spend on a host. I don't let them pay me. And no, this isn't part of my "company" job. This is part of my job as a human being. I'm not the best emcee. I've just found this is a way I can give back to my community. I also volunteer to help after ice storms by picking up debris or sometimes Greg and I spend the day helping family with household chores. One day people may not ask for me or us, but for now, this is something I can do, we can do. You will find your way. You'll reach a point where it becomes a balance of time for yourself, your family, and others.

We all go through different phases in our lives. One day, Greg and I hope to have kids. We will find a way to incorporate helping others into their lives. My sister has done an incredible job with this. I've already gone to several events with her that raise money for different things, such as the Susan G. Komen Race for the Cure in Tulsa. Holly brought my oldest niece. Three generations participated along with others. It was an incredible experience. My sister's children go to a wonderful school, and my sister is one of those who works tirelessly to help it grow by volunteering her time.

I also have to say that the Ozark Affiliate of the Susan G. Komen for the Cure foundation has changed my life too. Alison Levin is the director, and she has become a dear friend. I learn from everyone associated with this organization. We try to help them raise awareness about this disease through "Team Neile." We have has raised thousands of dollars in honor of my grandmother and every other family out there going through this disease. I now produce a show that runs anywhere from an hour to two hours every year for this event. My parents always drive over. My friend Sarah usually meets me when it's still dark out so we can walk or run the course and so I can make my call time for the live show.

I then anchor covered in sweat, and yes, Phong sometimes comes too.

I found by taking cameras with me for my mammogram and showing the whole process on the air, it seems to have encouraged others out there to get their mammograms.

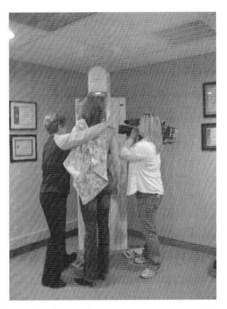

Neile Jones-Batie gets her mammogram and then shares the experience on television with KNWA viewers.

I try every day to do my job and at the same time give something back to the community that gives so much to others. I don't do anything more than anyone else. I am just in a place in my life where I can hopefully give a voice to issues and people who feel they have no voice.

Here is the deal. You have a chance at a fresh start, at real happiness. You have a chance to find out what made you choose this person or allow this person to choose you. You have time to stop and think, focus. What do you want out of life? I married the man of my dreams. I know what love means now. We are not perfect, but we love each other.

I swam a two-mile open water swim. I spent months in training for this.

I began working to give back to others though various projects. Below you'll find some pictures from various events, fun times that have allowed me to meet people and do things I never dreamed of until after I found myself again. I competed in a fitness competition. In fact, the first year I took fourth in my class; the next, third.

Neile Jones-Batie at Arkansas State Championship Competition; picture taken by Mark Mason

I wrote this book and have even started on a pilot's license.

Congressman John Boozman nominated me to the Women in Leadership Summit in Washington, DC, where I met some incredible people. I have been able to experience so many new things and meet different inspirational people and leaders because I made a choice to live my life rather than live in fear.

Photo by Eric Molle, PictureNWA.com as Neile Jones-Batie throws out first pitch at a NWA Naturals Baseball game

Neile Jones-Batie with LPGA player Cristie Kerr

Neile Jones–Batie interviews LPGA player Natalie Gulbis

Neile Jones–Batie with Bernadine P. Healy, MD
Health Editor U.S. News and World Report

Neile Jones-Batie with Carly Fiorina, Chairman
and CEO, Carly Fiorina Enterprises; friends
Patti Burcham and Jennifer LaPerre

Neile Jones-Batie with Coleman Peterson, presi-
dent and CEO of Hollis Enterprises, LLC

Neile Jones-Batie with US Senator Kay Bailey Hutchinson

Neile Jones-Batie with former President Bill Clinton

Neile Jones-Batie with Rachael Ray

Neile Jones-Batie with Stacy London

You can do anything if you believe you deserve those opportunities. I prayed for a man like my husband, for my heart to heal, and for God to show me what story I was supposed to tell. I believe this book could be the beginning of that story. But that is a story that's impossible to share without including my family. Later in this book you'll find thoughts from the heroes of my life: my family and friends.

I have to say about working and learning from these types of situations that none of us is perfect. We are all humans. The key for me has been to find the upside of humanity, appreciate your gifts and blessings, and never give up.

Your Light

If you let someone, they can try to put out the light that makes you "you." I began to realize that what makes us all unique isn't controlled by someone else. I believe everyone has a light inside. I always think of the song I sang in church as a kid: "This Little Light of Mine." The light, for me, is God's love. It is what makes you who you are. I believe it's what makes you able to love others.

Sometimes we get in our own way. We focus too much on what hurts, on the cruel or the hard. But if you can let yourself see the light, see what a blessing life is, you can share that with others.

I didn't have the most difficult situation. I didn't have the easiest. But what I did have and do have was and is faith in God's unconditional love. I mean, let's face it. I'm so imperfect it's not even funny, but I am one of God's creatures. So are you. So is Richard. The person who hurt you isn't perfect. You are not perfect. You can dwell on the hardships dealt to you or find the light inside and let it shine. Follow your heart to a peaceful place. Pray for forgiveness for the person who hurt you. Pray for forgiveness for yourself. It's not something you earn, but it's a gift you can share. I won't forget what happened in that relationship, but I have forgiven both him and myself. I also focus on the good, meaning the struggle of that time made the happiness of now even more great because I appreciate life more.

I married my husband, Greg Batie, in 2006. When we chose music, I picked "This Little Light of Mine" to walk down the aisle to Greg. I remember hearing the organist and smiling as if to wink at God and say, "Thank you." I see Greg's light every day with his every kindness. His light shines bright and in fact, helps me strengthen mine. We pray together, and we love together. I don't know what the future holds for you or us. I can only tell you that I try every day to be the best person I can be; some days I do much better than others. Still, I know each day is a gift with an opportunity to do more. And I am at peace with that concept. I look at my husband, and I see a blessing here on earth. Yes, we disagree. No, he's not perfect either, and that's the beauty of us. We don't have to be perfect. We love each other and all our imperfections without hate, resentment, fear—without abuse. He is my best friend even on his worst day, and on his worst day, I am his best friend. I have learned that a disagreement with the man you love doesn't mean you get hit. Greg is strong in every way, and he is a true gentleman. He is a Christian. He is my biggest supporter. We both make mistakes, but we work through them together.

I have come to a place where I listen to the people

around me who truly love me and who know I'll make my own choices in the end. But somehow they will always be there loving me, scars and all.

If you are in a bad relationship, pray, go to counseling, and figure it out. Get professional help, and make plans for an exit strategy. Find the light; it's there, but you have to remember to believe in what you may have forgotten. Believe in you. No parent, family member, or friend can make this type of decision for you. Only you can do the work. I can tell you that for many, it will be a choice between life and death. I hope you'll choose to live.

I believe in you!

I believe in you just as someone else believed in me. You can share the same gift with someone else. All you have to do is believe.

The last few pages of this book are blank for you. Write down what you want to change. Set some goals. Who should you contact? What do you need? Be careful and consult with a professional that can help you find the best plan possible for your situation.

From Father to Father

Neile Jones-Batie with her father, Sam Jones. Picture taken by Lori Staedke

In "A Week on the Concord and Merrimack Rivers, Wednesday," Henry David Thoreau wrote, "It takes two to speak the truth, one to speak and another to hear." What you are holding is a book in which our younger daughter speaks, and you've heard of the chilling, frightful, and tragically abusive relationship she broke free of. Neile shared with you the story of what appeared on the surface to be a perfect, loving relationship between two young people so lost in one another that nothing could ever come between them. But something did and that "something" came calling after they seemed to settle into a life based on the give and take that a relationship requires of two young people.

Unknown to her mother and me, or her sister, with whom she is very close, it began as emotional abuse and escalated into physical abuse. It was also unknown to her friends and associates in the town in which she lived. In other words, Neile faced the problem alone. She faced the pain of the abuse and what she perceived as failure on her part to make a relationship work. When the truth finally came out, the anger, guilt, and loathing slammed into all who knew and loved her and a protective circle immediately formed around her. I must confess that although years have passed, time has not healed my anger and guilt. But the direction of the anger has changed. Now it is not anger at the mental man/child who used her for a punching bag. It is anger at myself and my personal guilt for not knowing or recognizing the clues that should have been so obvious. Had I just taken the time to pay more attention... Sometimes both emotions come walking down the hall late at night, climb up on my bed, and sit on my pillow. When that happens, I get up and put on the coffee and wait for the sun because I know there will be no sleep that night. There are still elements of her experience

Neile Jones-Batie

I can't and won't talk about. In many respects, I'm no different from any other father, in that some wounds are too deep and I'll always regret not being there for her when she needed someone to dash into a phone booth, change into his daddy suit, and fly away with her in his arms. How Neile handled an abusive relationship and where she is now is what you are holding. I suggest you read it, put it down for a few weeks, and then read it again. If anything she describes from that relationship sounds familiar—either from firsthand experience or if it can be applied to a family member or friend—get involved. Help is out there. But first, like Neile, you or the person you love has to make a decision. It could save your life.

From Mother to Mother

Neile Jones with Grandmother Klober and mother, Linda Jones, at The Komen Ozark Race for the Cure

Someone has once said that having a daughter is like watching your heart walk around outside your body. This is so true with my daughters and granddaughters. From time to time, I had questions about things I observed in Neile's relationship, but she assured me that everything was fine. We first knew of the problems in reality when we received a phone call shortly after our weekend getaway to celebrate my husband's sixtieth birthday. We were all devastated with the news. A person was talking on the phone whom I had never heard before, in a voice filled with hurt, pain, and uncontrollable tears. This was my heart feeling the pain with this wonderful daughter who now felt she could no longer try to hold it all together. She had tried for over a year. One of my first questions to her was why she felt she had to endure this for even a minute. She explained why she felt she just had to make it work. We wanted her home safe above all else. She agreed, took time off from her work, and came home.

This lovely woman appeared at our door—broken, swollen faced, red eyed—with her beloved dog. We had questions but tried to just listen, hug her, and assure her that as long as she was safe, she had done the right thing. The first several days she just stayed alone in her old room and did not eat for the most part. Toward the end of the week, she began to rally and got up to eat some and take a shower, doing some normal things. She told us she could not go back. We were relieved she came to this decision.

For the most part, I could not share feelings with my husband, Neile's father. He became enraged and vengeful, a father's instinctive role to protect his daughter. I tried to help him focus on what we could do for our daughter and make her our focus. I began talking to a therapist who was a friend and a coworker at the time. This wonderful friend made me aware of the patterns in domestic abuse. She had previously been a counselor for Domestic Violence Intervention Services. She allowed me to vent without becoming judgmental or emotional. She also shared written material and pamphlets to further educate me, our family, and most of all, Neile. Neile read them all, I think, and used the knowledge to educate herself and protect herself against this vicious cycle that can be perpetuated if not dealt with in an assertive, affirming way. She continued in therapy during this challenging time.

I am a therapist, and I have realized in hindsight that I went through all the stages of grief and loss. I was in disbelief at first that this could have happened in what had begun as such a lovely time—I thought. I was angry then and needed to calm myself because this did not help me or our darling girl. Then I thought all those bargaining things: What if I had ... ? Why didn't I ... ? I am a professional. Why didn't I see it? etc. I suppose these thoughts are normal, but they are not useful for sure. They could keep me in a cycle of blame and feeling worse and worse. I then felt very depressed. I wondered what family, friends, church members, the minister would say. I was not giving any of them enough credit. With minimal information, they were all supportive for Neile's safety and emotional and physical wellbeing. The covenant she had made in such good faith had been broken—by another person. There was no choice other than to make decisions that would support her safety and well being. Everyone worked to that end.

Then I reached acceptance—"this is where we are, for whatever reason." As in most grief and loss situations, I wake at times in the morning or middle of the night in one of those stages, but I try to shake it off with positive thinking and much prayer.

After Neile returned to work and began legal proceedings, she came back home frequently and spent weekends with us. She had much love and support from us, her sister, her brother-in-law, and her niece. I loved being able to love and support her in this time. After several months, she began to visit with her friends, spend quality time with her sister and extended family, and seemed on a path to gradually returning to her life.

What has resulted from all of this is our Neile being in a wonderful marriage, feeling happy, and being a contributor in many different ways for the prevention of domestic violence and support for the victims. I think all of us surrounding Neile have a better understanding of how these things happen and realize that they happen to all races, classes, and groups of families. I strongly encourage anyone with even a suspicion of domestic violence or experiencing it to first be sure the at-risk persons are made safe and then contact the local DVIS (Domestic Violence Intervention Services) agency.

I cannot say that I am grateful for this experience. I have been able to pray that the others involved in this situation get the help they need. I do feel that we are closer as a family. We have our moments; we are a normal family with many varying opinions, but we deeply love each other, and I think this experience made all of us more aware of that love.

From Sister to Sister

*Neile Jones–Batie with sister, Holly Raley;
picture taken by Lori Staedke*

A person who appears to others to be in a bad relationship must decide that he or she is in a bad relationship before being receptive toward any initiative at making a change. Friends and family can offer assistance in this process. But ultimately the person in the bad relationship must hit the breaking point. As an older sister watching all this play out, this was a difficult role. The older sister is the one who is supposed to protect and guide, almost as a back-up mother, but be a friend too. Being objective about the guys the little sister dates is always hard because a big sister will scrutinize even a guy who is perceived to be the best for the little sister, a big sister will scrutinize until the final moment they say "I do."

When I first met Richard, I never would have thought this person would be "the one" for her. I would not have pictured this person being the father of her kids and the person who would grow old with her. I can't put my finger on exactly why. My opinion had nothing to do with anything visible or spoken, just a vibe. I convinced myself that if this was the person who made her happy, even if it was not the person I pictured for her, I must accept him. I decided that I needed to get to know this person better to try to understand what she felt. I even challenged myself to evaluate my criteria for who I thought would be the best person for her.

Along the way there were signs that things weren't peachy between them. As the relationship got more serious, I noticed she began to come home almost every weekend, most of the time without him. Most new couples I have known are attached at the hip, almost to the point of being nauseating to watch. She became very codependent on our parents for companionship and advice, in a manner that seemed out of balance. Again, I wondered if this was how she pictured it would be—her life, that is. It was not what I pictured for her, but maybe I was the one who had misjudged what she wanted from a relationship.

Maybe my initial vibe was right, but it was too late now for that to change the negative impact the situation had on her. The hardest part about watching a loved one hurt is the knowledge that she must go through that process to heal. She will need to sort out why she allowed it to happen and most importantly, how to break the cycle so it never happens again. The healing process cannot be rushed, and no one can do the healing for her. Friends and family must be patient. But when she emerges, she will be stronger and wiser.

While the end of a commitment is bad, staying in a bad relationship is worse. Once she ended things, I knew she needed a support system to help untangle the emotional web of hurt she experienced in that relationship. I am proud of her for having the courage to get out. I know she was concerned about the stigma of several things and wondered if people would judge her status. In the end, our family thought she was very brave. I hope that now that she is out of this she can close this chapter of her life, learn from it, and move on. Yes, it is a part of her past, but it is over.

From a Friend before and After

I first met Neile Jones when we were both working crazy early hours and I was new to the job. In true Neile fashion, she welcomed me to the company with a big smile and open arms. She played a key role in getting me up and running, and she did it with a great attitude, despite my lack of knowledge and the early mornings. To an outsider, Neile had it all. She was happy, she loved her job, and she was motivated, but it didn't take long for Neile to reveal her true self. When the cameras went off and the job was done, the "real" Neile started to show, the girl desperately trying to make it. Neile was trying to make it through the day. Neile was trying to be happy. Neile was trying to be motivated, but there was a dark cloud and secret unhappiness that Neile was *trying* to hide.

Over the months and then the years, Neile's and my relationship turned from a working team to a friendship. I knew there were days something was bothering my friend. There were days when she seemed on edge (so *not* Neile), and instead of prying and butting in, I tried to make her laugh. After building a friendship of trust, Neile started to open up. Even in her times of turmoil and fear, Neile was careful when talking badly about anyone. She still looks at the very best in anyone, but the secrets that had been haunting her were changing the warm friend that greeted me when we first met. She was desperate to find true happiness so she could stop pretending to be happy.

As a friend in this situation, there is not a handbook to tell you how to reach out or how to guide a friend through this dark time, so instead we prayed, we laughed, and we focused on the positives in life. Since Neile does like to keep her personal life private, I didn't know all she was facing. But I knew she simply needed a friend, and I tried my best to be that for her. So, as Neile began to realize she didn't need to live in her situation, the true Neile really started to shine. Whenever she would consider making a life change, we discussed it, and instead of telling her what to do, I encouraged her to be the best Neile she knew how to be. Before long, she had a plan, and eventually we were moving her to a different location and assuring her she was safe. The day she moved seemed surreal, but the friend I'd grown to love over the years was instantly a whole new person. Instead of *trying* to be happy, she was happy. Instead of *trying* to make it through the day, she just did it. Instead of *trying* to be motivated, she was a go-getter. The smile that so many people appreciate about Neile was now real instead of a mask. And instead of trying to please everyone else around her, Neile was focused on herself. But she wasn't focusing on herself in an egotistical way; she was finding the woman she'd let others control and change. Neile was coming out of her shell. Don't be fooled; there were hard days. There were lots of tears and lots of anger, but a determination to live life to the fullest, and if you meet Neile today, she is doing just that! You would never know the rocky road she took to get where she is today, but in an effort to reach others, she is honest about that journey. As her friend, I couldn't put myself in her shoes, I couldn't imagine her pain and fears, but I *could* (and can) encourage her. If you have a friend going through this battle, or any struggle for that matter, I encourage you to simply listen and encourage.

Still to this day, Neile thanks me for helping her through that tough time, and I normally just laugh. As her friend, I didn't do much. Yes, I helped move boxes and grab a tissue for her every now and then, but that's not what made her decide to say enough is enough. Usually I just listened and prayed, and it was Neile who realized (on her own) that she deserved better. It's been several years since Neile decided she was done being the victim, but she's not done sending a message. Neile is stronger than most know, and I'm privileged to know the true strength of my friend. She's a fighter. She'll make it through anything, and I'm proud to call her my friend. It's my friend who is going to reach others who are living the secret Neile was quiet about for too long. She'll admit she's not perfect and she made mistakes, but she's determined to let others know they're *not* alone.

The journey to this point has been eventful, to say the least, but I know I wouldn't—and I don't think Neile would—change a thing. If you were to meet Neile today, you'd never know she struggled with a secret; you'd never know that at one point in her life she was a victim; you'd never know she used to feel useless and inadequate; you'd never know she felt like a failure because today Neile shines. Neile lives life to the fullest, she is a fighter, she is powerful, she is a winner and achiever, she loves others, she is a giver, and she is an example. I know it hasn't always been easy, but Neile is the type of person to "go big or go home," so I know by writing this book she is determined to reach at least one person. And I am proud to say she is my friend because through her darker days, she reaches so many others by simply encouraging them to seek help.

—Sydney Yazwinski

A Word from My Husband

Neile Jones–Batie with husband, Greg Batie. Picture taken by Lori Staedke

Neile asked me to write this section in the hopes of being an outlet for other men who are in a relationship with a woman who has been through abuse.

First, I am not perfect, not even close. I have anger, can yell if pushed, and don't really like to see that side of me. We are guys; we want to fix everything that is thrown in front of us. We want to be the protector, the hero that saves the day. We want to be needed and respected. And most of all, we want to bring safety and comfort to our mates.

Now you're going to think that I am crazy but none of that matters. When Neile and I started dating, I could tell that she had been treated in a bad way. She was beaten down and having to work hard on trusting me to not be that same guy. I, by being the "man," could not make Neile trust me. I could not "fix" her. I could not protect her from her nightmares. I could not make her respect me or feel comfort with me. All of this happened, but over time.

After dating for about three months, Neile and I got into an argument. Nothing strange here; just a typical couple's argument. She was in the other room, and I was talking loudly, in my opinion, and she was doing the same. After about five minutes of being quiet, I started to wonder where she was. I had not heard the door open. Her car was still there. Where had she gone? I found her in the closet. Not hanging up clothes. Not organizing for the week to come, but rather hiding—hiding underneath a pile of clothes, crying. When I reached for her, she jumped in a way that I will never forget. She cried, "Please don't hurt me. I'm sorry." She expected me to respond in a way that I cannot even imagine. She was truly scared for her life. I still cannot remember what we were discussing. I can promise you it was not that important that she should be worried for her safety.

You are going to face things you cannot even imagine. As humans, we hope that all of us would share the same respect for fellow men and women. The person before me had one purpose: to control. You can take the easy way out and leave, say, "Man, that girl has issues," and go away. In some cases, that may be the best option for both of you. The reality is she does have issues. But if she means anything to you and if you can see someone inside who could be special to you, I promise you it is worth the effort to help. Neile and I have been married for over three years now. I am blessed. But if we were not married, not dating, just friends, I know that I would have a great friend in Neile and that I would be happy that I took the time to try to help her understand that not all men are about control.

In order for this to work, you are going to have to be willing to accept some strange times—times when you just want to go push the previous guy down the stairs and watch him bounce. It is not the way. That is what you are fighting. Early in our relationship, Neile and I had just finished up dinner and went shopping for televisions. We had had a great night up to that point, held hands as we walked into the store. All of a sudden I could not feel my fingers because she was squeezing so hard. My first response was to find this person who could put such a scare in Neile and be done with it. But I didn't. I said, "Let's go," turned around, and walked out. Later I found out that he was walking right toward us. I didn't even see him.

That time has passed. He does not have that control over her anymore. Neile has seen him with me and has been firm in the fact that we will not back down. It's not a duel. It is that she has just as much right to be where she is as he does. She doesn't fight, but she also doesn't run. Neile has learned how to trust and believe in someone. I hope to be able to care, love, respect, nurture, and support her as much as she does for me.

In closing, I would like to say to all of the men out there, we are strong. We want to fix. We want solutions. None of this will help until you are able to let your lady know that you are there for her. The best medicine that I can offer is a slow, deliberate hug and comfort. She may push you away, but remember: this is not you. Be yourself and let her know that she is not alone and that you are there to support her.

Neil Diamond Moment

Music has played a big role in my life. I love Neil Diamond. My family loves Neil Diamond. I think I've seen him in concert ten times. Neil Diamond's "I Am I Said" (written by Neil Diamond) has always been a song that I loved. My favorite version is on Hot August Night II.

As a woman who went through the "mirror" moment, I understand this song more than ever.

I've heard him talk about this song in interviews, and I know what it meant to him. For me, this song represents knowing what it's like to feel as if you are screaming on the inside to get someone to care about you and your talents but then realizing if you know what you can do, no one can stop you from living your dreams but you. I know what it's like to say, "Look at me; take a chance on me," and have no one listen. I also know that when you become comfortable with being alone with your own thoughts and when you can hear your cry, you can evolve into a peace that gives you strength for the moment when your chance to shine truly comes. Thank you, Neil Diamond.

For my family, not many memories come without a Neil Diamond song. My sister and I grew up listening to his music, and take a good look at my name. Notice anything?

I took Greg with my family to a concert in Tulsa—my parents, Greg and I, Holly and Kevin. We all sat together, along with my Aunt Nancy. We danced to every song and sang every word and probably drove everyone around us crazy. I looked at my husband, and I started to cry. I felt as though this was a moment I would never forget—my family together, laughing, singing, and dancing to music we'd grown up with. Greg smiled and hugged me as if he knew what was happening.

There was a time in my life when I thought moments like this one would never exist for me. I thought I'd never find someone worth introducing to my family. I thought I'd never love again. Here I was with a man I didn't deserve. Like most blessings, I am overwhelmed when I let myself think about him and the gift of love God has given us. Greg is a blessing. This night with family was a dream come true. Still to this day I sometimes cry when my family is together, whether it be my side of the family or Greg's side of the family. I cry not because I am sad. I cry because I am overwhelmed with joy and at the second chance God helped me give myself. I love this man more than I can say. I love this life. I can't believe I have such a wonderful family that would stand by me in the thick of it all—behind me, beside me, with me.

My wish for you is that one day you will sit with your family and friends and know the feeling of what it means to appreciate the struggle that has made your life better. I don't mean that in a condescending manner. I just mean to say I wish you joy, and I wish you peace with who you are, where you have been, and where you are going.

Thank You

To my dearest friends and family, when I needed you, all of you were there for me. I am blessed to have you all as friends. I'll never be able to repay you. I'll never be able to adequately thank you, but I will always love you. And maybe for a woman I never meet or you never meet, we can help her see that life goes on, love doesn't mean hitting, and real friends can't be replaced. In case I've not said it enough, thank you for helping me to see me and find myself when I was so lost even the mirror offered a tainted reflection. It may not mean much, but each of you and your families have some very special gifts, and I am grateful you have shared those gifts with me!

To Bridget: Thank you for all the times you sat with me and listened. You are a wonderful friend, and I love you. Sometimes in life you are just blessed to be around women with huge hearts. You are wonderful and beautiful in every way. Thank you for your friendship.

To Tom: Thank you for the wonderful pictures and for sharing your skills and talent with us.

To Kellye: Thank you for being my friend since we were kids and for all your love and support.

To Robyn and Eddie: I can't thank you enough for giving me a place to stay when I was most scared in my life. You are the kindest of people and exemplify the true meaning of selflessness. I love you both and your families for every kindness you've ever shown me and my family.

To Lisa and Ryan: Thank you, my friends, for helping me get back on my feet, for understanding the love I have for Phong, and for giving us both love when we needed it most.

To Sarah P. and your family: You are so incredible and are always there when I need you. Thank you for allowing me to be your friend and for being my friend.

To John, Rhonda, Kerry and your families: You make me laugh and help me be a better person every time I'm with you. Thank you for your friendship and for not giving up on me. Thanks for being my friends and for the wonderful people you are. I love ya!

To Jennifer: You asked a question that helped me leave. You asked in the most kind way. Thank you for being my friend, Jen, and for being supportive when I needed you most.

To Sydney: You are a blessing to all who know you. I think back on all those days when you sang, danced, joked— you always found a way to make me smile. Thank you for this friendship. I know you say you didn't do anything, but that's not true. You were a friend. You are a friend. I love ya!

To My movers—Tom, Sydney, Greg, Steve, Jimmy,

Diane, Uncle Stacey, Dad: You showed up and picked me up when I couldn't stand. You packed boxes and moved me from a scary place to a safe and secure home. I will never be able to express the feeling of seeing you—my friends and family—that day. We didn't call you, we didn't ask; you just came. You will always hold a special place in my heart because I know I can never repay you for your bravery and selflessness. Thank you for everything!

To my wonderful friends I've known since childhood and your families—Tina and Ryan, Kari and Chris, Chris and Kim, Drew and Missy, Lisa and Jon, and Amy V: I am so blessed to know you all. Thank you for loving me and all my imperfections. I am inspired by you daily and grateful to call you friends and family. Thank you for being there for me in the hardest of times and in the happiest of times. Thank you for being who you are and letting me be a part of your lives.

To Dr. and Mrs. Biggs: My family searched for a church home when we moved to Tulsa. We found it at Boston Ave. because of you and all the wonderful people in the congregation who have shown us love and compassion all our lives. Thank you for giving so many so much of you.

To Stephanie: Thank you for helping me finish a two-mile swim that with every stroke helped me want to learn more and do more for others.

My Hogeye Team: You knew how important it was to cross that finish line, and you stayed with me every step of the way. Thank you, my friends!

Sarah: Thank you for going to the dollar store with a total stranger who just wanted to offer you friendship like so many had offered her. You are the most beautiful sweet, inspiring, talented, loving person. Thank you for sharing yourself, your family, and Aub with me. And thank you for a friendship that will last forever.

To Eric: Thank you for sharing your talents with all of us.

To Susan and family: Thank you for encouraging me with this project and for your love, support, and friendship.

To Peaches and Coleman: I can't thank you enough for the support and friendship you've given our family. We love you guys!

To Alison and Dick: Thank you for being our friends and for teaching us every day about how to be better people. You are wonderful.

To Blake and family: When I was ready to quit, you wouldn't let me. When I thought I had nothing left to give, you proved me wrong. Thank you for believing in a girl so lost she just wanted to go home. People like you are a rare breed. You believed in me when I couldn't, when most bosses would have kicked me out the door without a second thought. You gave me a chance. Even better, you gave me your friendship. And thanks, Blake, for telling me to "get a life" and go out with that man ... who is now my husband.

To Susana: I am amazed by you and all your talents. Thank you for being my friend and for helping me achieve my dreams. You are a woman we all can learn from because you are honest and have an integrity that's not always easy to find. Thanks for seeing in me what I couldn't always see in myself.

To Scott: Thank you for always helping me and being such a great friend to us—even though you still owe us a golf game!

To Carrie: Thank you for all your love and support girl!

To María: Gracias por el regalo de tu amistad. Usted está sorprendiendo y I Love you.

To Marvin and Jennifer: Thank you for being our wonderful friends and for all your love and support.

To Betsy: Thank you for your friendship and trust. I love ya girl.

To the Trammels: Thank you for your love and friendship and for setting a great example for those around you.

To Torri: Thank you for your friendship and always helping me look and feel my best. You work wonders, girl!

To Missy: Thank you for your friendship and for helping me take care of my skin and myself. I appreciate you and all that you are and all that you do.

To my workout friends: Ladies, you are so strong inside and out. Thank you for helping me work harder on myself, even when I'm tired and just want chocolate.

To Jon: Thank you, bud, for helping me to keep going and for being my wonderful friend.

To Bruce: I came to you and said, "I want to be strong from the inside out." Thank you for helping me and getting me in perhaps the best shape of my life. You've been a great friend and motivator.

To Doug and Jennifer: We are so blessed to have you in our family. Thank you for loving us unconditionally.

To my aunts and uncles—Saunders, Jones, Batie, Sumners, Brady, Bundy, Gramlich, Jones, Klober, Meeks, Tidwell, Renos—and all my cousins; all my extended family: You are the best family, and we love you all and thank you for your friendship and love as well!

To Big Stacey: Thank you for your honesty and bravery. I love you, ya big turkey!

To Jody B. and John G.: Thank you for making me go on walks, for listening to me, and for sharing brother-like friendships with me.

To our law enforcement officers, attorneys, judges, legislatures, advocates, shelter directors and volunteers who try to help others find peace: Thank you for what you do every day to help people.

To David, Mike, Steve, Jennifer, Verleen, Brian, and Edith: Thank you for giving me my first job at an Arkansas television station. You made every day fun, and I am grateful for you all.

To Mike, Lisa, Matt, James, Brook, Rob, Dan, Aaron—okay, I'm going to stop because I don't want leave anyone out—and the rest of my KNWA/Nexstar family: Thank you for the opportunities you have given me, the friendship we share, and this wonderful television station in Northwest Arkansas that just won't give up. I learn from each of you every day. Greg and I love you all and your families.

To Matt: I am honored to call you my friend. Thank you for all the support and friendship. You are an amazing person with an inner strength that inspires all of us. We love you and Julee very much and thank you for your friendship.

To our neighbors: We are so grateful to live in a community that truly cares. Thank you all for your love, support, and friendship.

To all of our extended friends and family: Thank you for loving us and being supportive all our lives. We love you all!

To the Rice family: You change the world and make it

a better place every day just by being you. Thank you for loving us and being our friends and for helping us focus on what's inside all of us, the ability to be better.

To Elise: You are one of those amazing women that helps us all become better people. Thank you for your friendship.

To Kim: Thank you for believing in this project and for all you do to help others every day.

To James: I needed you, and you were there, man. Thank you for the respect you showed our family and for your wonderful friendship.

To Mr. S.: Greg and I love you and appreciate you and all you have done to help us grow.

To Jana: Girl you know I love you thank you for everything and keep up that scrap-booking!

To Kori and Jason: You have many special gifts and we are blessed that you share them with all of us.

To David: Thank you for all you do to help so many.

To Kara: You are a beautiful and wonderful person and I love ya girl!

To Alexa: I am so grateful for your friendship and can't tell you enough how much you mean to me. Thank you for being you and for being my friend.

To McKenna, Leah, Tristan, and Piper: You are all blessings from heaven above. You will always be our special nieces and nephew.

To The Batie, Blue, Lockhart, & Weaver families: Thank you for welcoming me into your family. We love you all.

To Kevin: Thank you for loving my sister and being

such a great husband, brother-in-law, and father to my nieces. I love you, bud.

To the Raley family: Thank you for all your love and friendship.

Mom and Dad, I love you. I wouldn't change anything about the way you've loved me. We've been through good times and bad, but no matter what has happened in life, I've had something many people never know: two parents who've done their best even through the darkest of days. Please know I love you, and I can't thank you enough for all your sacrifices, hard work, friendship, and life lessons. You are wonderful just the way you are. Mom, you are the sweetest woman I've ever known, both as a mother and a friend. Dad, you can be hardheaded and stubborn, but when I needed your arms around me with love and friendship, you were always there. I love you both just the way you are! Please remember that you did everything right when I needed you most. You are the reason I could find my courage.

To my sister, Holly, I can't talk about that time in my life without thinking of you. There is something about a big sister and her love and friendship that nothing in this world can replace. You may not know it, but I will always believe that you and Mom and Dad saved my life in many ways. You are a wonderful mother, talented woman, gifted human and beautiful person. You are still the sister who hands me her ice cream cone when I drop mine. Every woman should be so blessed to have a sister who is also a friend and mentor.

To my husband, Greg, you are the love of my life. Thank you for holding me after nightmares, for laughing *with* me instead of *at* me, for supporting me in every way a wife and friend should be supported, and for letting me support you. You are a gift from Heaven, and not a day goes by that I don't thank God, Greg Batie. You help me see ways I can be a better person just by being you. Your humility, strength, integrity, and courage are traits I learn from every day. My dad used to walk over to me when he could see I was hurting, and he'd just put his arms around me and say, "Neile, he's coming. He's out there, honey; don't give up." Dad knew I had to find me before I could find you. My dad was right, and you were more than worth the wait. You are a gentleman in a time when many have forgotten what that means. You are my bumblebee. I love you, Gregory. And I always will love you.

Most importantly, to God: Thank you for this life and all of its blessings.

Journal

_____

_____

_____

_____

_____

_____

_____

_____

_____

Look Again . . . Because You Can

Look Again . . . Because You Can

Helpful Resources

If you are in immediate danger, call 911. If are you are trying to formulate a plan to leave your situation, please contact the proper professionals to help you with that plan. I am just sharing my story; I'm not an expert, and everyone's situation is different. Remember, many experts say the most dangerous time for a person in a domestic violence situation can be when he or she is trying to leave.

National

American Domestic Violence Crisis Line
(Americans living overseas)
3300 NW 185th #133, Portland, OR 97229
Phone 1–866–879–6636
www.866uswomen.org

The Corporate Alliance to End Partner Violence
2416 East Washington Street, Suite E
Bloomington, IL 61704
Phone: 309–664–0667
Fax: 309–664–0747
Email: caepv@caepv.org
http://www.caepv.org/

The National Coalition Against Domestic Violence
NCADV's Main Office
1120 Lincoln Street, Suite #1603
Denver, CO 80203
Phone: (303) 839–1852
TTY: (303) 839–8459
Fax: (303) 831–9251
Email: mainoffice@ncadv.org

NCADV's Public Policy Office
1100 H Street NW
Washington, DC 20005
Phone: 202–745–1211
TTY: 202–745–2042
Fax: 202–785–8576
Email: publicpolicy@ncadv.org
http://www.ncavd.org/

UNIFEM
(703) 236–1535
www.unifem-usnc.org

The US National Committee for UNIFEM advocates for and fund raises to support the work of the United Nations Development Fund for Women, one of whose major goals is to end violence against women, including domestic violence, child brides, and rape as a weapon of war. UNIFEM has at any given time over 100 projects in developing countries designed to empower.

Arkansas

The Arkansas Coalition Against Domestic Violence
U.S. hotline 800–799–SAFE (7233)
http://www.domesticpeace.com/

Teen Dating Abuse Helpline:
866–331–9474

Peace At Home Family Shelter
P. O. Box 1923
Fayetteville, AR 72702
Phone: 479–444–8310
Fax: 479–587–1817
Hotline: 479–442–9811
Toll free: 877–442–9811
Web: www.peaceathomeshelter.com

Northwest Arkansas Women's Shelter
P.O. Box 1059
Rogers, AR 72712
Phone: 479–246–9999 (office)
Fax: 479–246–7072
Hotline: 479–273–0730
Toll free: 800–775–9011
Web: http://www.nwawomensshelter.org

Women and Children First
P. O. Box 1954
Little Rock, AR 72203
Phone: 501–376–3219
Fax: 501–376–4720
Hotline: 800–332–4443 Toll free
http://www.wcfarkansas.org

State Coalition List

(Can be found at
http://www.ncadv.org/resources/StateCoalitionList.php)

Alabama Coalition Against Domestic Violence
P.O. Box 4762
Montgomery, AL 36101
(334) 832–4842 Fax: (334) 832–4803
(800) 650–6522 Hotline
Website: www.acadv.org
Email: info@acadv.org

Alaska Network on Domestic and Sexual Violence
130 Seward Street, Room 209
Juneau, AK 99801
(907) 586–3650 Fax: (907) 463–4493
Website: www.andvsa.org
Email: info@andvsa.org

Arizona Coalition Against Domestic Violence
301 East Bethany Home Road, Suite C194
Phoenix, AZ 85012
(602) 279–2900 Fax: (602) 279–2980
(800) 782–6400 Nationwide
Website: www.azadv.org
Email: acadv@azadv.org

Arkansas Coalition Against Domestic Violence
1401 West Capitol Avenue, Suite 170
Little Rock, AR 72201
(501) 907–5612 Fax: (501) 907–5618
(800) 269–4668 Nationwide
Website: www.domesticpeace.com
Email: kbangert@domesticpeace.com

California Partnership to End Domestic Violence
P.O. Box 1798
Sacramento, CA 95812
(916) 444–7163 Fax: (916) 444–7165
(800) 524–4765 Nationwide
Website: www.cpedv.org
Email: info@cpedv.org

Colorado Coalition Against Domestic Violence
1120 Lincoln Street, Suite 900
Denver, CO 80203
(303) 831–9632 Fax: (303) 832–7067
(888) 778–7091
Website: www.ccadv.org

Connecticut Coalition Against Domestic Violence
90 Pitkin Street
East Hartford, CT 06108
(860) 282–7899 Fax: (860) 282–7892
(888) 774–2900 In State DV Hotline
Website: www.ctcadv.org
Email: info@ctcadv.org

Delaware Coalition Against Domestic Violence
100 West 10th Street, #703
Wilmington, DE 19801
(302) 658–2958 Fax: (302) 658–5049
(800) 701–0456 Statewide
Website: www.dcadv.org
Email: dcadv@dcadv.org

DC Coalition Against Domestic Violence
5 Thomas Circle Northwest
Washington, DC 20005
(202) 299–1181 Fax: (202) 299–1193
Website: www.dccadv.org
Email: info@dccadv.org

Florida Coalition Against Domestic Violence
425 Office Plaza
Tallahassee, FL 32301
(850) 425–2749 Fax: (850) 425–3091
(850) 621–4202 TDD
(800) 500–1119 In State
Website: www.fcadv.org

Georgia Coalition Against Domestic Violence
114 New Street, Suite B
Decatur, GA 30030
(404) 209–0280 Fax: (404) 766–3800
(800) 334–2836 Crisis Line
Website: www.gcadv.org
Email: info@gcadv.org

Hawaii State Coalition Against Domestic Violence
716 Umi Street, Suite 210
Honolulu, HI 96819–2337
(808) 832–9316 Fax: (808) 841–6028
Website: www.hscadv.org
Email: admin@hscadv.org

Idaho Coalition Against Sexual and Domestic Violence
300 Mallard Drive, Suite 130
Boise, ID 83706
(208) 384–0419 Fax: (208) 331–0687
(888) 293–6118 Nationwide
Website: www.idvsa.org
Email: thecoalition@idvsa.org

Illinois Coalition Against Domestic Violence
801 South 11th Street
Springfield, IL 62703
(217) 789–2830 Fax: (217) 789–1939
(217) 242–0376 TTY
Website: www.ilcadv.org
Email: ilcadv@ilcadv.org

Indiana Coalition Against Domestic Violence
1915 West 18th Street
Indianapolis, IN 46202
(317) 917–3685 Fax: (317) 917–3695
(800) 332–7385 In State
Website: www.violenceresource.org
Email: icadv@violenceresource.org

Iowa Coalition Against Domestic Violence
515 - 28th Street, Suite 104
Des Moines, IA 50312
(515) 244–8028 Fax: (515) 244–7417
(800) 942–0333 In State Hotline
Website: www.icadv.org
Email: admin@icadv.org

Kansas Coalition Against Sexual and Domestic Violence
634 Southwest Harrison Street
Topeka, KS 66603
(785) 232–9784 Fax: (785) 266–1874
Website: www.kcsdv.org
Email: coalition@kcsdv.org

Kentucky Domestic Violence Association
P.O. Box 356
Frankfort, KY 40602
(502) 695–5382 Phone/Fax
Website: www.kdva.org
Email:kdvasac@aol.com

Louisiana Coalition Against Domestic Violence
P.O. Box 77308
Baton Rouge, LA 70879
(225) 752–1296 Fax: (225) 751–8927
Website: www.lcadv.org
Email:sheila@lcadv.org

Maine Coalition To End Domestic Violence
104 Sewall St.
Augusta, ME 04330
(207) 430–8334 Fax: (207) 430–8348
Website: www.mcedv.org
Email: info@mcedv.org

Maryland Network Against Domestic Violence
6911 Laurel-Bowie Road, Suite 309
Bowie, MD 20715
(301) 352–4574 Fax: (301) 809–0422
(800) 634–3577 Nationwide
Website: www.mnadv.org
Email: info@mnadv.org

Jane Doe, Inc./Massachusetts Coalition Against Sexual
Assault and Domestic Violence
14 Beacon Street, Suite 507
Boston, MA 02108
(617) 248–0922 Fax: (617) 248–0902
(617) 263–2200 TTY/TDD
Website: www.janedoe.org
Email: info@janedoe.org

Michigan Coalition Against Domestic and Sexual Violence
3893 Okemos Road, Suite B-2
Okemos, MI 48864
(517) 347–7000 Phone/TTY Fax: (517) 248–0902
Website: www.mcadsv.org
Email: general@mcadsv.org

Minnesota Coalition For Battered Women
590 Park Street, Suite 410
St. Paul, MN 55103
(651) 646–6177 Fax: (651) 646–1527
(651) 646–0994 Crisis Line
(800) 289–6177 Nationwide
Website: www.mcbw.org
Email: mcbw@mcbw.org

Mississippi Coalition Against Domestic Violence
P.O. Box 4703
Jackson, MS 39296
(601) 981–9196 Fax: (601) 981–2501
(800) 898–3234
Website: www.mcadv.org
Email: dvpolicy@mcadv.org

Missouri Coalition Against Domestic and Sexual Violence
718 East Capitol Avenue
Jefferson City, MO 65101
(573) 634–4161 Fax: (573) 636–3728
Website: www.mocadsv.org
Email: mocadsv@mocadsv.org

Montana Coalition Against Domestic & Sexual Violence
P.O. Box 818
Helena, MT 59624
(406) 443–7794 Fax: (406) 443–7818
(888) 404–7794 Nationwide
Website: www.mcadsv.com
Email: mcadsv@mt.net

Nebraska Domestic Violence Sexual Assault Coalition
1000 "O" Street, Suite 102
Lincoln, NE 68508
(402) 476–6256 Fax: (402) 476–6806
(800) 876–6238 In State Hotline
(877) 215–0167 Spanish Hotline
Website: www.ndvsac.org
Email: help@ndvsac.org

Nevada Network Against Domestic Violence
220 South Rock Boulevard
Reno, NV 89502
(775) 828–1115 Fax: (775) 828–9911
(800) 500–1556 In State Hotline
Website: www.nnadv.org
Email: nnadv@powernet.net

New Hampshire Coalition Against Domestic and Sexual Violence
P.O. Box 353
Concord, NH 03302
(603) 224–8893 Fax: (603) 228–6096
(866) 644–3574 In State
Website: www.nhcadsv.org
Email: mattern@nhcadsv.org

New Jersey Coalition for Battered Women
1670 Whitehorse Hamilton Square
Trenton, NJ 08690
(609) 584–8107 Fax: (609) 584–9750
(800) 572–7233 In State
Website: www.njcbw.org
Email: info@njcbw.org

New Mexico Coalition Against Domestic Violence
201 Coal Avenue Southwest
Albuquerque, NM 87102
(505) 246–9240 Fax: (505) 246–9434
(800) 773–3645 In State
Website: www.nmcadv.org
Email: info@nmcadv.org

Neile Jones-Batie

New York State Coalition Against Domestic Violence
350 New Scotland Avenue
Albany, NY 12054
(518) 482–5464 Fax: (518) 482–3807
(800) 942–6906 English-In State
(800) 942–6908 Spanish-In State
Website: www.nyscadv.org
Email: nyscadv@nyscadv.org

North Carolina Coalition Against Domestic Violence
123 West Main Street, Suite 700
Durham, NC 27701
(919) 956–9124 Fax: (919) 682–1449
(888) 232–9124 Nation wide
Website: www.nccadv.org

North Dakota Council on Abused Women s Services
418 East Rosser Avenue, Suite 320
Bismark, ND 58501
(701) 255–6240 Fax: (701) 255–1904
(888) 255–6240 Nationwide
Website: www.ndcaws.org
Email: ndcaws@ndcaws.org

Action Ohio Coalition For Battered Women
5900 Roche Drive, Suite 445
Columbus, OH 43229
(614) 825–0551 Fax: (614) 825–0673
(888) 622–9315 In State
Website: www.actionohio.org
Email: actionoh@sbcglobal.net

Ohio Domestic Violence Network
4807 Evanswood Drive, Suite 201
Columbus, OH 43229
(614) 781–9651 Fax: (614) 781–9652
(614) 781–9654 TTY
(800) 934–9840
Website: www.odvn.org
Email: info@odvn.org

Oklahoma Coalition Against Domestic Violence and
Sexual Assault
3815 North Sante Fe Avenue, Suite 124
Oklahoma City, OK 73118
(405) 524–0700 Fax: (405) 524–0711
Website: www.ocadvsa.org

Oregon Coalition Against Domestic and Sexual Violence
380 Southeast Spokane Street, Suite 100
Portland, OR 97202
(503) 230–1951 Fax: (503) 230–1973
(877) 230–1951
Website: www.ocadsv.com
Email: adminasst@ocadsv.com

Pennsylvania Coalition Against Domestic Violence
6400 Flank Drive, Suite 1300
Harrisburg, PA 17112
(717) 545–6400 Fax: (717) 545–9456
(800) 932–4632 Nationwide
Website: www.pcadv.org

The Office of Women Advocates
Box 11382
Fernandez Juancus Station
Santurce, PR 00910
(787) 721–7676 Fax: (787) 725–9248

Rhode Island Coalition Against Domestic Violence
422 Post Road, Suite 202
Warwick, RI 02888
(401) 467–9940 Fax: (401) 467–9943
(800) 494–8100 In State
Website: www.ricadv.org
Email: ricadv@ricadv.org

South Carolina Coalition Against Domestic Violence
and Sexual Assault
P.O. Box 7776
Columbia, SC 29202
(803) 256–2900 Fax: (803) 256–1030
(800) 260–9293 Nationwide
Website: www.sccadvasa.org

South Dakota Coalition Against Domestic Violence &
Sexual Assault
P.O. Box 141
Pierre, SD 57501
(605) 945–0869 Fax: (605) 945–0870
(800) 572–9196 Nationwide
Website: www.southdakotacoalition.org
Email: pierre@sdcadvsa.org

Tennessee Coalition Against Domestic and Sexual Violence
2 International Plaza Drive, Suite 425
Nashville, TN 37217
(615) 386–9406 Fax: (615) 383–2967
(800) 289–9018 In State
Website: www.tcadsv.org
Email: tcadsv@tcadsv.org

Texas Council On Family Violence
P.O. Box 161810
Austin, TX 78716
(512) 794–1133 Fax: (512) 794–1199
Website: www.tcfv.org
Utah Domestic Violence Council
205 North 400 West
Salt Lake City, UT 84103
(801) 521–5544 Fax: (801) 521–5548
Website: www.udvac.org

Vermont Network Against Domestic Violence and Sexual
Assault
P.O. Box 405
Montpelier, VT 05601
(802) 223–1302 Fax: (802) 223–6943
(802) 223–1115 TTY
Website: www.vtnetwork.org
Email: info@vtnetwork.org

Women's Coalition of St. Croix
Box 2734
Christiansted
St. Croix, VI 00822
(340) 773–9272 Fax: (340) 773–9062
Website: www.wcstx.com
Email: wcsc@pennswoods.net

Virginians Against Domestic Violence
2850 Sandy Bay Road, Suite 101
Williamsburg, VA 23185
(757) 221–0990 Fax: (757) 229–1553
(800) 838–8238 Nationwide
Website: www.vadv.org
Email: vadv@tni.net

Washington State Coalition Against Domestic Violence
711 Capitol Way, Suite Suite 702
Olympia, WA 98501
(360) 586–1022 Fax: (360) 586–1024
(360) 586–1029 TTY

1402 Third Avenue, Suite 406
Seattle, WA 98101
(206) 389–2515 Fax: (206) 389–2520
(800) 886–2880 In State
(206) 389–2900 TTY
Website: www.wscadv.org
Email: wscadv@wscadv.org

Washington State Native American Coalition Against Domestic and Sexual Assault
P.O. Box 13260
Olympia, WA 98508
(360) 352–3120 Fax: (360) 357–3858
(888) 352–3120
Website: www.womenspiritcoalition.org

West Virginia Coalition Against Domestic Violence
5004 Elk River Road South
Elkview, WV 25071
(304) 965–3552 Fax: (304) 965–3572
Website: www.wvcadv.org

Wisconsin Coalition Against Domestic Violence
307 South Paterson Street, Suite 1
Madison, WI 53703
(608) 255–0539 Fax: (608) 255–3560
Website: www.wcadv.org
Email: wcadv@wcadv.org

Wyoming Coalition Against Domestic Violence and Sexual Assault
P.O. Box 236
409 South Fourth Street
Laramie, WY 82073
(307) 755–5481 Fax: (307) 755–5482
(800) 990–3877 Nationwide
Website: www.wyomingdvsa.org
Email: info@mail.wyomingdvsa.org